Forward

The effectiveness of your communication determines the effectiveness of your life. Leaders who people respect and follow are those who are able to communicate effectively. They have a dynamic presence. If you desire to make a difference, learn to communicate with a powerful presence. You must be able to communicate what you want to get done in the church, in the ministry, and in life.

The pulpit is no greater than the person who fills it on a weekly basis. If the preacher is boring to the congregation, the people will think God is boring. Some ministers have style without substance while others have substance without style. Preachers need to be able to combine substance with style in their communication. The Christian and non-Christian alike are searching for truth in a generation preoccupied with self, avarice, and greed.

In *Blockbuster Storytelling*, Robb Hawks has combined his global knowledge of the Church with his professional experience of decades of ministry. Over the years, I have heard ministers say, "I sure wish I could preach or teach like Jesus!" Yet, they very seldom apply the adjustments necessary to achieve this communication goal. Missionary Hawks gives to us an understanding of the substance needed and the style required for listeners to truly "hear" the minister's message.

Substance is "what" is said and style is "how" it is said. There is a certain amount of style in the packaging of a message. In John 12:49, Jesus said, "For I did not speak on my own initiative, but the Father Himself who sent me has given me commandment, what to say, and what to speak." In other words, Jesus was led by the Father in all aspects of His speaking engagements.

When you read, *Blockbuster Storytelling*, you will come face-to-face with a renown communicator who has impacted more than 100 million people through his dynamic stories; each developed and delivered in a life-saving manner. You will learn how to combine substance and style in order to more effectively preach/teach like Jesus.

The communicator is to deliver into the possession of the person for whom it was intended. Delivery refers to the methods by which you communicate "what" you have to say to the "who." Many souls are not saved because the sermon was never delivered to the lost. It is possible for the preacher to speak the message, use up a portion of time, give an invitation, and still not accomplish the intended purpose of the sermon.

I am grateful that Robb has chosen to bring *Blockbuster Storytelling* to the center stage of lives to persuade us to learn how to tell stories for the salvation of untold millions in the years ahead.

Dr. James O. Davis
Founder/Cutting Edge International
Cofounder/Billion Soul
January, 2013

Also by Robb Hawks

The Prime Directive

Winds of Adventure

The Prince of Babylon

Understanding Why

Dynamics of Church Growth

The Notebook: The Children's Worker Handbook

The Adventures of Billy Adams

The Captain's Logbook

Dive Log

Blockbuster Storytelling

By Robb Hawks

For my son, Robby.

He loves telling stories as much as I do.

Table of Contents

Story

Everyone loves a good story. We read them, watch them, listen to them, and sometimes are a part of them. Stories happen all around us every day. We tell them to each other, share them on line, and offer our opinions as armchair quarterbacks. The human being is prewired, that is genetically programmed, for storying. This is how we process information and remember things.

2002 World Memory Champion Andy Bell uses an interesting method to allow him to remember the order of 10 decks of playing cards in only 20 minutes. Think about that! He can memorize the order of 520 cards! How is this possible? Is he a super genius? He does not attribute his amazing skill to some supernatural talent. Andy says that he trained his memory using a technique that I recognize as leveraging the human mind's innate power to story. His technique is rather simple. First Andy memorizes a simple route through town. Most of us do this all the time. Some of us create a map in our mind where we picture the roads and how they fit together, while others memorize landmarks along the route. I draw maps in my mind, while my wife memorizes the landmarks. Andy creates his route using landmarks.

Next, he associates a character or object with each playing card. For example, a jack of clubs might be a bear, a nine of diamonds a saw, and a two of spades a pineapple. The route and the characters have been memorized long ago so he does not need to concentrate on them. When it comes time to memorized decks of cards, Andy looks at the first three cards in the deck and begins to *create a story* that will allow him to remember the cards. He will remember the jack of clubs, the nine of diamonds, and the two of spades by creating a story of a bear (jack of clubs) using a saw (nine of diamonds) to cut a pineapple (two of spades) in half at the first landmark on his route. He continues this process, drawing together 3 cards at a time, into mini--stories that happen in succession as he walks along the landmarks of his route. He creates an adventure with a cast of characters in each setting!

Humankind stored its wisdom and history in spoken stories for many millenniums. We call these people groups Oral Societies. They have an oral history and oral culture. Storytellers play a significant role within oral societies. Grandparents and the elderly are widely respected as they remember the truths, history, and values of the culture passing them on to future generations in their stories.

Each story has a truth, proverb, or teaching associated with it. Over time the truth and the story become synonymous. Hearing the story for the first time, the young learn the associated truth. For those who know the story, they immediate think of the truth. This works in reverse as well. Mention the truth and immediately everyone remembers the story.

"Slow and steady wins the race." Immediately this brings to mind Aesop's fable about the tortoise and the hare. But it also works in reverse. Mention "The Tortoise and the Hare" and what comes to your mind? "Slow and steady wins the race!" **Story telling has the power to create mental images that eternalize truth.**

Relationships are crucial among Oral Societies. Tribes, families, close and distant relatives are simultaneously the focus and method of communication. Small towns still maintain some of the roots of oral societies where everyone knows everyone's business and news travels faster than the speed of light! Much of the world still would be considered oral. Although there may be a baseline of literacy, the society still operates as a traditional oral society. In parts of Africa knowledge has value and thus is prized and leveraged to advantage. For example, a friend says that he is looking for three men to work in his business. This knowledge has value. There is money to be made. Rather than share this information with just anyone, the recipient of the information would carefully repeat it only to family so that the employment and the profit therein is "kept in the family."

While working with a translator in Africa we were surprised at how little information he would give us. We would ask questions in regard to schedule, route, equipment, or contacts and we consistently were given very little information. This puzzled us until we began to understand the culture. The information was being held close. As long as the translator knew these things he was valuable to us and his continued employment was guaranteed.

Does all of this sound somewhat familiar? Most of civilization falls into an oral society culture in one form or another. It is our instinct. We have to be trained to think differently and even then, we relapse into orality at a moment's notice.

Modern western society has worked feverishly to change culture from oral to written. A by-product of this is that we have codified knowledge into structured outlines and formal arguments. But given a chance to choose, even highly educated and literate western society will plop down in front of their TV and watch a story. This is how we were created. **Humankind is first and foremost storytellers.** Whether it is a half dozen Maasai women of Kenya standing around the well or six office workers in New York standing around the water cooler; you know they will be gossiping and telling stories. You won't find much conversation based upon formal higher critical thinking around the 'watering hole.'

Let's face it, *we all are instinctive story tellers-it's in our DNA.* Ask any parent who has confronted their child about some less than desirable conduct. Children have an amazing capacity to make up a story. Adults are no different. When called on the carpet by their supervisor the subordinate's mind rushes into story mode. Isn't that what Adam did when confronted by God in the Garden of Eden? Adam told God a story blaming it all on the woman. We are all innate storytellers. We have to be trained to think in linear arguments.

Powerful stories expressed eloquently have the ability to evoke strong emotions and motivate us to action. Madison Avenue marketing companies have leveraged this truth into a multi-billion dollar industry. Television ads tend to fall into a few categories. The first is the simplest and I think least effective. These are the ads where a product or service is explained and the options and benefits are touted. People who are in the market to purchase the product are merely informed but rarely inspired to action. Then there are the ads that tell a story. These 30 second miracles are designed to evoke emotion and motivate the viewer to want to purchase the advertised item. Superbowl commercials are state-of-the-art. They have to be because advertisers spend up to 3.5 million dollars for a 30 second commercial. *That's $167,667 per second!*

The 2012 top 10 Superbowl commercials were all stories. Not a single one concentrated on ticking off the many benefits of the product but rather created humorous stories with a punch line designed to evoke emotions and create long term visual images. After all, the advertisers want the audience to remember the ad and product. It is difficult to remember a list of facts but easy to remember a story.

Television and motion pictures are the ultimate form of storytelling in media literate societies around the world. Billions of dollars are spent each year creating programs to earn huge profits and simultaneously project a liberal Godless theology. Its 'success' has made the behavior of the immoral Hollywood sub-culture the norm. Just like advertisers understand the power of changing the individual's product preference through advertising, Hollywood has embedded its liberal agenda into the fabric of the programs it produces.

The percentage of babies conceived out of marriage in 1980 was double that of 1950. This statistic exploded between 1970 and 1988 when never-married mothers were the head of 248,000 households in 1970 and by 1988 never-married mothers were the head of 2,700,000 households -- a ten-fold increase! By 2010 we find an unbelievable condition in American society: 29% of white children, 53% of Latinos, and 73% of black children are born to unmarried women. How could such a radical change take place in such a short span? Part of the explanation is found in the stories told and consumed by society.

So, humankind is preprogrammed to stories, advertisers sell using stories, TV and film makers make billions telling stories, *and preachers stand up in front of their congregations and spout three point sermons and expect to change the world.*

It is tragic that the church has the greatest "product" the world has ever known and yet embraces the less-than-ideal delivery method of the "structured sermon." When we consider who teaches our pastors to preach, this is understandable. Young pastors go to seminary where they are trained by academics who teach "higher critical" thinking.

Within this group traditional sermon structure is a refined and understood art. But these young pastors will not be preaching to academics, but rather to John Q. Public who couldn't care less about critical thinking and he sure does love a good story. As Solomon said, "there is nothing new under the sun." During Jesus' time the Pharisees, (the lawyers of the day), spouted argument, legal theory, and written opinion.

Jesus on the other hand, told stories.

I grew up in church. Some of my earliest memories were falling asleep under my mother's pew as the pastor preached his heart out. These were the days when you attended Sunday morning and evening, and again on Wednesday night. No one-hour service would satisfy in those days. Church was an experience that typically lasted a minimum of two hours. The only preaching I remember from my childhood was when the evangelist came to town and told incredible stories.

Years later I would face the challenge of standing in the pulpit myself and preach many a message in hope of moving the congregation. Sermon after sermon was structured correctly according to what I had been taught in Bible College. But it didn't take long for me to begin to read my audience and discover that I wasn't keeping their attention from beginning to end. They perked up and became engaged in my message as I told stories to illustrate principles, and then their eyes would glaze over as I hammered away at my outline and arguments. Albert Einstein said that the definition of insanity is to continue to do something the same way and expect a different result. I decided that I wanted different results when I preached and I would do something different to get those results.

Pastor Paul Graban was my pastor in Burlington, New Jersey when I was a child. One day, as a young man just starting out in life, I asked for his advice. "Find someone successful, and do what they do!" he replied. Great advice that on occasion comes to the forefront of my mind to challenge me. I began to analyze the preaching style of some of the church's great ministers. They all had one thing in common; they could all tell a story. When this truth suddenly burst into the proverbial "ahah!" moment, it became obvious to me that I must learn to tell stories and incorporate them into my preaching style.

Then God threw me a curveball. I was hired at a large church to be a children's pastor! For the next 11 years I told story after story after story. Don't be fooled into thinking children are easy. They are brutally honest, with short attention spans. If you lose them in your story telling they don't sit quietly and respectfully. First you see it in their eyes as they check out and then they begin to fidget in their chairs. Soon you lose control. Not a pleasant situation. But a great way to hone your story telling skills.

Then one day I was asked to evaluate a kid's TV show. This led to writing and producing the stories/scripts for a series of TV shows. These programs were produced and translated into numerous languages and broadcast to over 100 million viewers worldwide. No one wanted to broadcast my 3-point sermons! But through my stories, my Gospel has been preached to an incredible number of people. The power of story!

There are many types of stories. Most jokes are short stories giving a lot of bang and emotional effect for just a few minutes of investment. Every pastor relies upon jokes or humorous short stories in his sermon.

The documentary is another form of story. Documentaries range from short "news" stories up to feature length films. Typically documentaries are told from an event perspective, linking together a series of events that the viewer might find interesting. Although they can be intellectually stimulating, they typically never achieve broad viewership or acclaim. Unfortunately, most pastors use the documentary style to tell stories from the Bible. They tackle the content with a series of statements explaining events in which the Bible characters are added. This might be a great method to deliver factual information but it typically falls short of capturing the listener's imagination and thus does not usually evoke strong emotions. Think of a witness in a trial relating a series of factual events to describe an accident or crime. At first it is interesting, but soon you are snoozing.

Hollywood refined the art of storytelling and along the way a number of unofficial rules were developed which govern scriptwriting. Follow the rules and you have a chance at a profitable film. Break the rules and you will probably lose your shirt. Follow the rules, add some creativity, hire a great team, and you just might have a blockbuster!

I have taught Hollywood scriptwriting at a number of colleges around the world. We analyzed blockbuster films and discovered they all follow certain rules. We can adapt these rules when preparing our stories. After all, a blockbuster movie is nothing more than a story told really well.

What is a story?

A story is about people, not places or events. Our listeners are drawn to the human element. Great stories have great characters we can relate to and aspire to be like.

Imagine a massive thunderstorm dumping rain upon a dry desert. The rain falls faster than the earth can absorb it, thus streams form that flow into a river that soon becomes a raging torrent. The river cuts through the desert floor, forming a valley with steep cliffs on either side. The fast moving water erodes the underside of the cliffs and soon an entire side of the towering wall of the valley collapses. Dramatic. But nothing that will get you on the edge of your seat.

Now consider John and Ruth, a handsome young couple obviously in love, each sitting in a kayak working their way down the raging river together. John knows that Ruth loves the adventure of kayaking. There is a beautiful secluded spot with a spectacular waterfall just a few miles down the river. He plans on a romantic marriage proposal when they stop for lunch.

They paddle hard as the powerful currents nearly spin them around. John is leading, carefully picking a path to take them safely down the river, avoiding the underlying rocks. Unbeknown to him, the entire side of the cliff has become unstable. Cracks are beginning to form along its face. Faster and faster John and Ruth race down the muddy river. Neither of them aware that their lives are about to change forever. Suddenly, without warning, the cliff face gives way dumping tens of thousands of tons of rock and red clay into the river.

We now have two versions of this story. Both stories ended at the same place with the cliff falling into the river. Which story leaves the reader wanting more?

1. A story is about a Hero.

Good stories will revolve around a single hero. This is an important concept because it keeps the story focused. This does not mean that the story shouldn't have secondary characters. Most good stories do. But there needs to be a hero; a person the audience will bond with, relate to, and desire to see succeed.

We could tell the story of the Israelites having a war with the Philistines. We could talk about all the various characters. This is what is called an "ensemble" cast. A little of King Saul's story, a little of Samuel's story; we could even mix in a little of Goliath, the giant's, story. But the audience would have a difficult time getting personally involved. Who are the listeners supposed to care about? Why is one character's wants and needs more important than another's? But if we rewrite the story from David's perspective, suddenly there is a compelling hero to root for.

There were two movies released in 1998 that were incredibly similar in theme but were produced differently. Both movies focused on a large asteroid striking the earth and causing death and destruction. "Deep Impact" had an ensemble cast of many characters who each had their own stories. "Armageddon" had a hero, Bruce Willis, who drove the story. While both movies had great casts, amazing visual effects, and a huge budget, one had almost twice as many viewers and thus made twice as much money. "Deep Impact," with its ensemble cast, grossed $350 million worldwide while hero driven "Armageddon" grossed $554 million.

2. A story is about a Hero and what he wants.

A great story is always about a hero and what he wants. His want drives the story.

Having a worthy "want" is important. This is where the audience typically connects with the hero. One must believe that his want is worthy of the efforts that he will soon have to go through to achieve his "want." In "Deep Impact" the asteroid is heading towards the earth and it is apparent that there will be massive destruction. All the characters want to survive. There are a number of sub stories dealing with coming of age and relationships, but there is not a single driving storyline that grips the audience. The movie "Armageddon" is not really about an asteroid impact. It is about a father, Bruce Willis, and what he wants; his daughter to be happy. This relationship drives the entire human side of the film. There is actually a scene at the beginning of the movie where Bruce Willis comes right out and tells the audience that this is what he wants; his daughter to be happy. When the government approaches him to lead the mission to fly to the asteroid and destroy it, he doesn't want to go. He would rather someone else do it. But, the happiness and safety of his daughter drives him to do what he doesn't want to do. The audience buys into his reasoning. We want him to get what he wants. We want him to destroy the asteroid and save his daughter.

Returning to our story of David and Goliath, how could we frame this story so it is about a hero and what he wants? Perhaps we begin with David standing alongside his father as his brothers gather up their weapons to go to war against the Philistines. David wants to know why he can't go with them. His brothers tease him about being a runt and suggest that He needs to go take care of his sheep. As they exit to war, David tells his father that one day he will go to war and become a great hero.

Dad and brothers laugh, and David embarrassed, turns and walks away towards his sheep.

3. A story is about a hero who has a want and what he has to go through and overcome, to get what he wants.

This is the essence of a great story: A hero with a worthwhile desire, overcoming incredible odds and difficulties, to accomplish what he desires. Isn't this what every human desires: to get what he wants, to be a winner, to get the girl, to find the treasure, to defeat the enemy? Tell a story like this and you capture the imagination of all your listeners.

"Deep Impact" totally missed this crucial element. "Armageddon" nailed it right on the head. Bruce Willis overcame incredible difficulties to rescue his daughter and assure her happiness.

Let's look again at our Bible story, about David and Goliath. Now you may remember that things are not going well for Saul's army. Goliath comes out each afternoon with taunts and challenges someone to come and fight him. Meanwhile, David is frustrated and angry. He is out watching the sheep, slinging rocks at trees and shrubs as targets. David is not getting what he wants. He feels he has been left behind. Have you ever had that feeling before? Of course, everyone can relate to life passing them by. But then David's father calls him and gives him the task of carrying food to his brothers at the battlefield. Suddenly David might just get the opportunity he so desires. But you and I both know, he has a long way to go and numerous things to overcome before his fateful appointment with Goliath on the battlefield.

4. Great heroes are human.

They have weaknesses, flaws, and what some call, a wound. These must be overcome in order for the hero to get what he wants. He must grow and change and increase in order to face his challenge and get what he wants. In "Armageddon" Bruce Willis has a wound and a flaw. His failed marriage haunts him and he wants his daughter to do better than he had. Thus when he finds that his daughter has fallen in love with one of his young and irresponsible oil derrick rough necks, he becomes angry. This conflict constantly drives what he does and how he relates to his daughter. Willis believes that the boy is bad for her. But as the story unfolds slowly the father grows past his prejudice to see that his daughter truly loves the young man and that she will not be happy without him. The hero grows and the audience cheers him on.

Our hero, David, arrives at the battlefield. He is the youngest and smallest of the brothers. No one takes him seriously. He hears the taunts of Goliath and then asks what he would earn if he were to kill the giant. Most laugh and mock him, but word gets to King Saul and eventually, to everyone's surprise, David is brought before the king. What was going through David's mind? Is he really so full of faith that he thinks it will be no big deal to face the giant? We know that he tried on King Saul's armor, but he was too small for it to properly fit him. Will David be able to face his fear of being the baby and actually go out to face the giant?

A story is about a Hero: what he wants, what he has to do to get what he wants, and how he has to grow past his weaknesses, flaws and wound to finally achieve his desires.

The Villain

If every great story must have a hero, then every great story must have a villain! The proper term for the hero is the protagonist and the correct term for the villain is the antagonist. But down here in the trenches it's all about heroes and villains.

Great heroes require great villains. If the villain is too weak and too easily defeated, then the hero doesn't have to be a very good hero to get what he wants. Imagine the story of David and Goliath. Why are we all so enamored with this story? David, a wonderful hero with a great "want" faces an adversary that is twice as tall as him and who weighs four times as much! To create an even more imposing villain, we discover that Goliath has been trained in warfare from childhood. But even that is not enough! Goliath is covered in Philistine armor. His spear is more like a fence post and the sound of his deep voice causes tremors of terror to overcome the army of the Israelites. Now that is a villain! And our hero? Just a shepherd boy wearing sheepskin and carrying a sling.

1. Villains have a want.

All villains have a want that is in conflict with what the Hero wants. Perhaps they both want the same thing and only one of them can have it. This is the theme of 90% of all chick flicks. Two guys want the same girl. One is the hero, the other the villain.

Sometimes what the hero and villain want are diametrically opposed. For instance, Goliath wants to force all the Israelites to become Philistine slaves. David wants his people to remain free. It is impossible for both of them to get what they want.

2. Villains are bad.

Villains must be bad and described in such a way that the audience does not end up connecting to them and cheering them on to defeat the story's hero. This is not good for your story when everyone is rooting for the villain. Yet, on occasion, great actors playing villains "steal" the show. Thus, it is very important to quickly establish that the villain is offensive so the audience would prefer the villain be dead, in jail, or at the least, utterly defeated. This is usually accomplished by revealing something bad about the villain.

In the opening scene of the Academy Award winning movie, "The Gladiator" starring Russell Crowe, a war is about to take place. The Roman Legion led by Russell Crowe is ready to defeat the Germanic people in a very bloody battle scene. This type of gore and violence usually turns off the ladies in the theater. But the writers have done their job. A kind, white haired ambassador is sent by Russell Crowe to try to make peace with the Germans. Instead of peace, the leader of the Germanic tribes cuts the ambassador's head off and holding the bloody head high, he stands on the hillside taunting the Roman's. The audience instantly despises him. He has killed an innocent man! He deserves to die! So, when Russell Crowe and his Roman army attack and kill all the Germanic tribesmen, everyone cheers! It's just a scene later when you meet the real villain of the movie; the emperor's son. The writers did a wonderful job portraying him as an arrogant, condescending, spoiled child. I don't know anyone who liked him from the moment he appeared on screen!

Similarly, even in chick flicks, the villain is always exposed as being unfaithful, a liar, a cheat, or all the above. A villain must be a villain. And he must be a worthy opponent to boot. For example, think of all the things women hate in men and then put them into the villain of a chick flick movie.

3. Villains have a complete arsenal of weapons to defeat the hero.

Have you noticed that the bad guys always seem to know the hero's weakness? How is that Superman, who is impossible to defeat, always ends up fighting an enemy that somehow has managed to get a piece of Kryptonite? But this is an important part of storytelling.

The audience often connects or identifies with the hero's weakness or wound. In the word's of Bill Clinton, the audience "feels" the hero's pain. Thus we crave seeing the hero overcome his weakness. We desperately want him to grow. Why? Because deep down inside we all would like to grow through and past our own weaknesses and flaws. We overcome our own wounds vicariously through the hero. Thus, it is paramount that the villain challenges the hero in his point of weakness, forcing him to grow and become a better man.

Did you notice that the audience has a want? We want the hero to grow. We want the hero to succeed. We want the villain to lose. Just like the hero has a want, great story telling evokes a need or a want in the audience. Blockbuster storytelling first creates the want and then gives the audience what they want, resulting in a happy audience, who comes back for more!

4.   Villains often have an Achilles heel weakness.

The Greek hero Achilles was held by his heel and dipped into the River Styx, making him invincible. But his heel had never gone under water and thus was his only point of vulnerability. Achilles great fall was the result of a single arrow that struck his heel.

In the case of our villain, Goliath, he was arrogant. We know this because of the taunts he hurled at the Israelites. We also know this because he apparently was not wearing his helmet when he faced David on the battlefield. Almost all villains have a weakness or flaw that they do not grow through and ultimately results in their destruction.

Pride, anger, jealousy, deception, betrayal, greed (basically everything that is negative), can be the villain's weakness. Great stories always have a moral embedded in the sub-text of the story. When the villain is defeated because of his pride, the adage "Pride goes before a fall" is the embedded moral.

The Foundation

To build a great story it is essential to have a strong foundation for it to stand on. The premise, genre and setting are each foundation stones.

The Premise:

The premise is the one clear cogent thought or principle underlying truth of the story. The premise should be able to be stated in a single sentence. Its purpose is to keep the storyteller or writer on track. Without clearly understanding the premise, it is easy to get distracted and the story becomes muddled and lacks purpose.

The premise of J. R. R. Tolkien's Lord of the Rings might be stated like this: together friends can accomplish what the individual cannot. The premise of the Bible story of Saul & Samuel can be stated: to obey is better than sacrifice. The premise of the Bible story of Peter and the house of Cornelius: God loves and receives all people equally.

One must be careful with the premise. It is not meant to be a club with which to beat the listeners, nor is it meant to be a chain to restrict the storyteller. Rather it is the spinal cord, which connects the entire nervous system of the story.

Typically the premise is not stated in the story; but a well-crafted story leaves the audience to discover the premise.

The Genre:

Action adventure, romance, comedy, crime, thriller, documentary, fantasy, historical, mystery, sci-fi, morality, and religious are some of the genres available for today's storytellers. Each genre has general rules and descriptors that help define the story.

Some of these are obvious. **Action-adventure is the number one genre** of motion picture stories and is typically about a hero on some quest where he has to overcome incredible odds to get what he wants. Frodo Baggins becomes the reluctant hero of the Lord of the Rings trilogy. This epic is non-stop action with the hero in constant threat of death, or worse.

Romance is so formulaic that only the setting and the names of the characters seem to change. The love triangle is set within cultural context, molded by historic time period, international location, and socio-economic conflicts. But, it always comes down to a woman, a man, and the pursuit of love and happiness.

Most romance stories involve three primary characters, frequently two men and a woman (the heroine). One man is her perfect soul mate and the other is not. Romance stories are typically heavy on relationship and light on action. This is the number one genre among women.

Documentaries are dependent on reporting the facts and sequence of events or situations. These are not hero driven stories typically. Ensemble casts with characters that come and go as the events unfold leave the audience caught up in the events rather than identifying with the characters.   Documentaries are seldom blockbusters.

Morality and Religious stories are some of the most difficult to craft because the author has a message to convey to the audience. Often the message is not one the audience prefers to hear; thus the story can come across as a sermon and turn off the very people targeted. Morality stories typically end with a twist and the moral is presented at the end. Religious or message stories are best approached as a straight up story with the message embedded not in the text of the story, but rather in the sub-text.

In the USA, the gay rights movement has leveraged this concept to promote their agenda. Very few people choose to watch an openly gay movie. Thus a homosexual propaganda movie is not going to accomplish much. But Hollywood writes many stories and scripts where the gay agenda is in the sub-text of the story. Have you ever noticed that on some sit-coms most of the lead characters, although loveable, are extremely dysfunctional? Yet, there is often a secondary character that is the most normal person on the entire show.   This is the gay guy who lives in the next apartment and borrows a cup of flour. He, or rather his sexual orientation, is not crucial to the storyline. But, because he is 'normal' and accepted by the other characters as just the guy next door, the message embedded in the subtext of the story is that gays are normal and should be accepted. The writers did not have to preach to get their message out. Thirty years ago homosexual behavior was considered abnormal and deviant. Society has reached a critical moment, where after decades of messaging, it is politically correct to say that homosexuality is normal.

34

Actor Steven Seagal is considered one of the top 30 action-adventure stars of all time. But he is a passionate ecologist. While his early films were just plain fun, his later films became eco-warrior films and in some of them he lectures the audience! For me, this is a total turn off.

This should be a lesson well learned. Tell a great story. Do not preach or lecture. Embed your message in the subtext of your story, it will be widely heard and your message will have an impact.

Story Types

In each of the genres there is a subset of categories or story types. **The coming-of-age story is classic and is found in every genre.** Think about our story of David and Goliath. The genre is action-adventure and the story type is coming-of-age. In order to craft the story to effectively lead the audience on a satisfying experience, it is crucial to understand the story type. Remember, a story is about a hero, what he wants, and what he has to overcome to achieve it. What was it David wanted? He wanted to be a man and not be treated like a child anymore. This was his underlying motivation. Delivering Israel from the Philistines was the epic challenge he had to overcome to get what he wanted.

The story of Esther is another coming-of-age story. A young Jewish girl becomes the queen of an empire and must use her influence to save her people. We follow her from young teen to daring queen. This story could be told as a romance story where the young girl eventually falls in love with the king, while wicked Haman is set on destroying her and her people.

The story of young King Josiah, Solomon, and even Rehoboam can all be told as coming-of-age stories. It is important to remember that in the coming-of-age story the hero must make the transition from child or teen into adult.

Another story type is **the apprentice,** which is actually a variation of the coming-of-age story. In the apprentice we find a master and a student. The student must learn and overcome many challenges to go from apprentice to master. The original Star Wars trilogy was an action-adventure sci-fi coming-of-age story where Luke Skywalker was an apprentice and eventually became a Jedi Master. In every apprentice story the hero is faced with decisions that either make him or break him. These challenges are universal and the audience can relate to them. Luke Skywalker is challenged by his father, Darth Vader, to 'turn to the dark side'. In the Bible, Elisha was apprentice to Elijah. Peter was apprentice to Jesus. This is the universal challenge that every man faces, whether to resist temptation or give into carnal desires.

The "unlikely hero" is one of the most common and endearing story types. David was an unlikely hero. How can a young inexperienced shepherd deliver the people of Israel? Jael, the young Bedouin wife of Heber, delivers the Israelites from the oppression of General Sisera with a tent peg. In the blockbuster movie series "Transformers" Shia LaBeouf plays Sam Witwicky, a teenage boy who saves the world. In the famous J. R. R. Tolkien trilogy, "The Lord of the Rings," Frodo Baggins is the most unlikely hero. In all of these stories, ill equipped and normal individuals are suddenly cast into events that are way beyond their knowledge, ability, and experience. The audience is drawn into the 'unlikely hero' story because each of us hope to someday become a hero in our own right.

The Setting

A story's setting is usually crucial to the story. The setting encompasses the location, culture, society, moment in time, and a host of other small seemingly insignificant events such as like the weather, global events, and fashion.

There are three keys to success in the Real Estate business: Location, Location, and Location. This is also true in storytelling. Everyone knows the story of Jesus feeding the 5000. It is a favorite among children's workers around the world. The location of the story helps us understand why these events transpire. Jesus had set up a house in Capernaum as his base of operations for ministry in Galilee. It was extremely busy with people coming and going constantly. Capernaum was a fishing village on the northwest corner of the Sea of Galilee. The Sea of Galilee is actually just a big lake about 7.5 miles wide and 13 miles long. There were a number of villages along its shores and in the hills overlooking it. Fisherman rowed or sailed small boats, casting nets. They were hoping to catch schools of small fish to be salted down and sold at market. Down the coast from Capernaum was the city of Tiberius that was built by King Herod who had imprisoned Jesus' cousin, John the Baptist. Now during Jesus' time most of the villages were on the north, west and south shores of the Sea of Galilee.

There are some other details about the setting we should know. It is the time of Jesus, 2000 years ago, people didn't have cars, so they walked. During this time, Kings with great arbitrary power ruled. Powerful forces vied for the minds of men where religions clashed with national identity. So what really happened in the story of Jesus feeding the 5000?

Jesus and his disciples were in their base of operations in Capernaum. Peter and John's fishing boat was pulled up on the bank of the Sea. It was early in the morning when the disciples of John the Baptist showed up. They had not slept the night before. John the Baptist was beheaded by King Herod in Tiberius during a party the previous night. His disciples recovered his body and buried it. Then, with heavy hearts, they walked three hours up the coast to Capernaum to find Jesus.

The news of John's death deeply moved Jesus. John was his cousin, but perhaps of even greater significance, John was the very last prophet of the Old Covenant. Suddenly the busy chaos and commotion of his home became too much and Jesus decided he must get away and pray. Without making any significant preparations, he called his disciples, they boarded Peter and John's boat and began to row the five miles to the opposite shore. Jesus was going to a place in the wilderness to be alone to pray. It would take 2-3 hours to row this distance.

However, people on the bank noticed that Jesus and his friends were leaving. They called out to each other and followed the boat's progress by walking along the shore. As they walked the crowd grew. People came down out of the villages and joined the mob. While the disciples rowed 5 miles, the villagers had to walk 6-7 miles. The boat was only about 2 miles off shore at its greatest distance, so the crowd could easily follow. Now no one had planned for a day's walk or adventure. It was impromptu. Thus when Jesus reached the other side the crowd was waiting for him. And although he was in deep sorrow, he ministered to them and taught them. Of course, we now get to the crux of the story. They are in the wilderness, without food, with no villages nearby, and over 5000 very hungry people.

Jesus is about to perform a miracle. He will take a small boy's lunch and feed them all. What was in this lunch? Five loaves of bread? Well, sort of. Actually the loaves were not much more than dinner rolls. And the two fish were probably of the variety typical in the villages - small, thin, gutted and salted, head and fins included!

As you can see, the setting in this story is crucial to understand it. We could even back the story up a bit and include the beheading of John the Baptist. A view of the time period and cultural issues helps the audience understand the events that took place at the dinner party which led to John's beheading.

Storytellers dance along a razor sharp cliff. Too little setting and the story evolves without a backdrop, which can leave the audience confused. Too many details can bog the story down, sapping its energy and boring the audience.

The first Star Trek movie opened with an excessively long sequence of shots showing the new Starship Enterprise. 'Trekkies' loved it. But the regular audience quickly became bored with too much information that was not essential to the story.

Hollywood Formula ONE: Action Curve

Every great story follows a path leading to success. Stories that meander tend to get lost and never meet their true potential. There are six distinct parts in a great story: The Hook, Introduction, Establishing the Conflict, Building the Plot, Climax, and Resolve.

These 6 key components are like bones in a skeleton upon which everything else hangs.

The Hook

Hollywood discovered it is really easy to lose an audience; sometimes before you even have them! Both TV and film adopted a powerful tool to grip the audience and suck them in before they have a chance to tune out. This is called the Hook.

The idea is to "hook" your audience from the very first scene. We find this used extensively in TV dramas. "Law

and Order" perfected the hook. They show the first scene, typically the murder, even before the title and opening credits are played. The assumption is that if you can capture your audience's attention during the commercial break before they have a chance to switch channels, then they will stay tuned for the rest of the show. Many films also start with very dramatic scenes. The action sequences do not necessarily introduce the hero of the story. Sometimes they merely set up the situation or introduce the villain. One thing is for sure, the Hook is often mission critical for the story teller. It is like the first paragraph of a novel. Many authors labor for weeks to get the first line or paragraph perfect.

The Hook is very dramatic with high intensity or energy. It is like a sample taste, or a tease, of what is to come. Walking into a restaurant and smelling an intense and wonderful aroma is a hook. You can barely wait to sit down and eat. Even if you must wait 15 minutes to get a seat you never consider leaving because the smell has whet your appetite and you know the best is yet to come. So it is with an intense, well written and delivered hook. It's a taste that leaves the audience wanting more. They will sit on the edge of their seats waiting for the big payoff.

The Introduction

Every great story must have a thorough introduction. When did this story take place? Where is it taking place? Is the story happening now, 20 years in the past, or during the days of the Roman Empire? Is it in the city? Or perhaps it starts on a farm at the edge of the woods. Is it spring, summer, fall or during the

cold of winter? All of these aspects of the setting help the audience fill in the blanks of the story with their own imagination. It eases the burden of the storyteller, allowing him to concentrate on the action as opposed to describing the scenery.

During the introduction we typically meet the hero and through a series of events come to like him and want him to succeed. It is very important that the hero be introduced early. The audience is already on board, the hook has done its job, now it is time to figure out who the main characters are. Remember, unless the story is a sequel, this is the very first time the audience will meet your hero. There must be intentionality in every aspect of the first meeting with him. Who is he? What does he do? Is he likeable or is he a jerk? Why should I care about this character? What is there about him that I can relate to?

A good storyteller will use empathetic devices to help connect the hero to the audience. In film making these are often visual unspoken clues. The opening scene of the Academy Award winning film, "Gladiator", is a masterpiece. In this film, the Hook is merged with the Introduction. The Roman legion lines the valley with forests on both sides. The warriors prepare for battle. Many look tired. The great general enters. Suddenly the men snap to attention and show him respect. He nods and pauses as he walks along recognizing his men. It is obvious from their reactions that they like him. Why is this important? If the common warrior likes him, then he must be an okay guy, even if he is a general! As he passes by one rather aristocratic officer he stops and puts the man in his place. Again, the audience loves this. A hero who is a man of the people who will not give into pressure from his peers. Finally, a large German shepherd dog runs up and follows him. It doesn't get any better than this, if he is loved by a dog then he MUST be alright! It is crucial that the audience connect with this hero immediately because he is about to fight a battle with the Germanic tribes and hack and slash many people to their death. While the men in the audience may love the gruesome gore, the female half of the audience will not be so generous. Hence, it is imperative that the audience connects with the hero before the blood begins to flow.

Just as empathetic devices were used to connect the audience to the hero, negative-empathetic devices can turn the audience against the Germanic tribal leader whom the hero is about to kill. All of this in an exciting, punishing, and gory opening scene, i.e. The Hook.

In the Introduction we should be introduced to what it is the hero wants. It is very important to reveal "the want" early in the story to help the audience understand why the hero is doing what he is doing. In the opening scene of the "Gladiator," the hero, Maximus, is asked what he will do when this last battle is won? Maximus clearly states what he wants: to be with his wife and son. He repeats this a number of times throughout the film, thus keeping the audience in tune with what is driving him. His want never changes from the opening scene to resolve.

Establishing the Conflict

Stories without a clear conflict tend to meander towards a climax; a climax that the audience is not so sure it cares about. Remember, a story is about a hero, what he wants, and what he has to overcome to achieve what he wants. If there is no conflict or resistance to the hero, then what is the point? If the hero wants to win the state basketball championship and his team wins every game virtually uncontested, then although the hero gets what he wants, it wasn't very exciting getting there. Villains add conflict and challenge the hero to grow and overcome insurmountable obstacles to get what he wants.

Villains often make their first appearance towards the end of the introduction. Sometimes there is a face-to-face confrontation. In other situations the hero and villain are in different locations but heading on a path toward collision. In either case it is important to establish that there is a conflict. It will not be easy for the hero to get what he wants. In some cases his want will be virtually impossible and he will need help to achieve it.

The bottom line is this. Very quickly the audience must be Hooked, Introduced to the setting, identify with the Hero and his want, and then a Conflict must be established. All of this typically happens within the first 5-10 minutes of a film. In short stories this must happen within the first minute or two.

Developing the Plot

It is now time to get down to business and develop or "tell" the story. From the establishment of the Conflict the story mounts up a head of steam as the hero faces various challenges in his quest to get what he wants. Most spoken stories are limited to one or maybe two challenges that lead to the climax of the story.

The challenges that lie in the path of the hero take on many forms. The most common obstacle comes from the villain; however this is typically the last and culminating challenge of the story. But often a story has sub-challenges, such as resistance from family, friends, geography, or weather. In the story of David and Goliath, David faces numerous challenges before he faces the giant. First he is confined to the hillside to watch over the sheep while his brothers go off to war. This is overcome when his father sends him to the battle carrying food for his brothers. But once he makes it to the battlefield how does he transition from messenger to warrior? His own brothers laugh and scoff at him. He makes outlandish requests for information on what the person would earn as a reward for defeating the giant. Each of these must be overcome before he can take a shot at killing the giant. When telling a short story each challenge builds upon the previous one to increase the energy of the story as it races forward to the climax. In longer format stories, such as movies and novels, each challenge is more structured, with its own Hook, Intro, Conflict Establishment, Plot Building, Climax, and Resolve. The Resolve allows the audience to catch its breath as the story suddenly lurches forward into the next challenge.

The critical aspect of developing the plot is to build energy and tension as you push towards the Climax.

The Climax

The Climax is that magic moment when the hero gets what he wants and the audience jumps up out of their seats cheering! At least that is exactly what all storytellers hope will happen. It is very important that the hero gets what he wants. The audience first connected with the hero during the introduction and then discovered his want. Remember the hero's want drives the story. The audience has been rooting for the hero to get what he wants from almost the beginning of the story. If you go all the way through the story and the hero ends up not getting what he wants, the audience will feel short changed and will unlikely come back to hear your next story.

There are, however, a few exceptions to this rule. As the character grows and develops in the story his original want might be replaced with a more mature want.

There was a lonely treasure hunter who lived only to find the next treasure. He discovered a map and set out to find the treasure. Along the way he acquired a lovely assistant who fell in love with him; but he, being consumed with his treasure hunting, was oblivious. (As the story develops his feelings for her grow.) Together, they finally arrive at a cave where the final key to acquiring the treasure lies. With this key the hero will finally get what he wants. But just as he is about to grasp the key, there is an earthquake and the cave begins to collapse. His lovely assistant is trapped under a stone and he is faced with a decision: save the girl or get the key. Suddenly he realizes that he wants the girl much more than the key and turning his back on the key he rescues the girl.

In this example the hero gets the very thing he needed, yet didn't know at the beginning of the story he wanted. Of course the final scene of this story, the Resolve, ties up the loose ends. We find the hero with his girl walking out of the library with a new treasure map in hand setting off on their next adventure. This story's premise: treasure is temporal, but relationships, true love, are eternal.

Sometimes the hero must die in order to get what they want. In the "Gladiator," Maximus' wife and son are murdered; yet this was his want, to be with them. Throughout the film he is driven by only one thing. Return Rome to the people, thus fulfill his promise to the Emperor, and then be reunited with his wife and son. But there is no life or joy in his battle with the Emperor. Finally, he faces off with the evil Emperor in a battle to the death. Overcoming a crippling stab wound, and facing a determined foe, Maximus kills the villain and then collapses in the Coliseum. His childhood sweetheart rushes out to him, begging him not to die but to stay with her and together they will create a new Rome and new lives together. Suddenly she realizes this is not what he wants and she tells him to go to them. And with that we find Maximus walking through wheat fields with an open gate before him and there, walking down the trail towards the gate, is his wife and son. Thus, in death, the hero finally gets what he wants. And the audience is crying and boohooing. The hero is dead and we are happy for him!

Likewise in the movie Armageddon, Bruce Willis and his daughter's boyfriend are on an asteroid racing towards the earth. They have drilled a tunnel into the core of the asteroid and sent a thermonuclear warhead into the tunnel. Its explosion will destroy the asteroid and save the earth. But there is a problem. The detonator is broken. Someone will have to remain behind to manually set off the nuke. They draw straws and the boyfriend draws the wrong straw. He will have to die so that the world will be saved. But Willis has grown through the film and come to accept that his daughter loves the boy and that he is essential to her future happiness. So Willis sabotages the boy's spacesuit and takes his place. Willis stays behind to detonate the nuke, save the earth and take care of his daughter. The boyfriend and the team return to earth. Willis gets what he wants by securing his daughter's happiness and making sure that her boyfriend makes it safely home. And the earth is saved, even at the cost of his own life.

This concept of the hero getting what he wants by losing his own life is the story of the **life of Jesus.** He wants to redeem man from his sin. This is only possible if Jesus, God's sacrificial lamb, dies in mankind's place.

The Resolve

The Resolve is the shortest part of the story. It is where the loose ends are tied up leaving the audience satisfied.

It's like having a cup of coffee or desert after a wonderful meal. In the first Indiana Jones movie, "Raiders of the Lost Ark," Indiana Jones gets what he wants -- he finds the lost Ark of the Covenant. Through an amazing journey, he recovers it from the villain. The last scene of the movie has Indy and Miriam leaving the Federal building complaining that they are not being told what has happened to the Ark. The very last shot shows a crate being placed in a massive government warehouse. This is important since Indy Jones supposedly recovered the Ark during WWII, we the audience, would be left wondering where it was today. But the storyteller's answer is revealed in the Resolve. The storyteller wants the audience leaving satisfied and fulfilled. Like a good meal, they will be back for more.

We also find this to be true in the resolve of the movie "Armageddon." The hero is dead but the boyfriend has been reunited with the daughter. The last scene of the movie is their wedding. The daughter is happy, and Willis is there as a photograph, his want fulfilled, as his daughter's life becomes complete through her marriage. The audience has a good cry and is totally satisfied as they leave the theatre.

Just as the ocean releases its energy upon the shore in a rhythmic ebb and flow, a good story manages its energy to take the audience on a rollercoaster ride culminating in an exciting Climax. The chart below plots this energy through the 6 phases of a story.

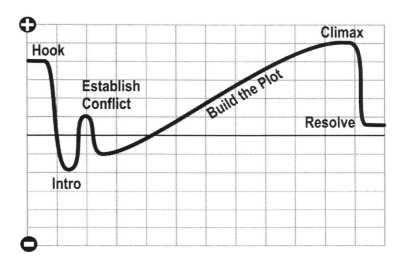

The Hook should be high energy. This can be fast moving action or a dark and intense situation. Either way, it is crucial to have the energy dial way up to slap the audience and get their attention.

During the Introduction the energy drops dramatically. There is a lot of ground to cover, people to meet and get to know, and often cultural or period principles to be slipped into the story for it to make sense as the plot unfolds.

As the villain is introduced and the Conflict established the energy or intensity rises again. Imagine two teens hurling insults at each other with the final outcome a promise to meet after school and settle the matter. Although there is not a lot of action per se, the moment is wrought with energy and tension. Thus our energy curve has a noticeable and dramatic up-tick as the conflict is set.

Now, it is time to build the plot. Just as our two students walk away from each, surrounded by their friends they make their way towards the first class period of the day, and the energy suddenly drops giving the audience a quick sigh of relief. Building the plot is like building a brick wall. You stack the bricks one upon the next. Slowly, but surely, the wall becomes higher and higher, reaching the point that all are sure it will collapse. Our teenagers go through the day with the 'after school fight' looming overhead. Friends offer advice. Our hero is taught a secret fighting move; that, if he can remember it, might just give him the advantage he needs. The lunchroom is fraught with danger. Our hero and the villain meet briefly and it looks like the fight will break out in the middle of the serving line. Cool heads prevail and friends pull the combatants away from each other. The villain sneers and threatens to kill our hero. The clock slowly moves from hour to hour, punctuated by the class bell, finally announcing that the fight is only minutes away. Along the way we discover things about our hero and the villain. We discover why the villain is such a bully and we also discover why our hero has been sucked into this conflict. We find that our hero is all heart but has little skill at fighting. An early childhood family conflict scarred him and left him incapable of standing up to bullies. Now, as he struggles to confront his fear and overcome the demons from his childhood, the moment of truth arrives.

The plot must build and continue to build in order for there to be sufficient energy to make the climax satisfactory.

Once the hero gets what he wants, the story reached its climax and as far as the audience is concerned, the sooner it is wrapped up the better. Thus the Resolve is very short and the energy level typically very mild. Perhaps one of the longest resolves every written or produced is the end of the "Lord of the Rings" movie trilogy. It seems to go on and on. While it does a great job of tying up loose ends and making its fans happy that there is still more movie even though we are way past the climax, the reality is that long resolves become anti-climatic and can leave the audience with an unpleasant aftertaste.

Hollywood Formula TWO: Emotion Curve

Just as the Energy Curve drives the story and keeps it moving forward to a satisfying and intense Climax, **the Emotion Curve is what determines a blockbuster.** You can craft your story and hit all the marks of the Energy Curve and have a good story. But our goal is not just a good story, but a Hollywood Blockbuster story.

The Emotion Curve is measured in either positive feelings of wellbeing or negative feelings that are experienced vicariously though the life and actions of the hero. Whereas the Action Curve is all about energy, action, and movement, the Emotion Curve is all about what the audience is feeling inside.

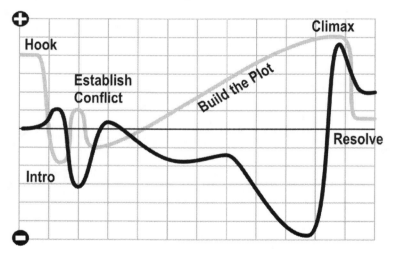

Remember the Emotion Curve is how the audience perceives the wellbeing of the hero. Thus, at the hook we typically don't know who the hero is; therefore we can't feel one way or another about him. Consequently, the Emotion Curve is neutral. But during the intro we meet the hero and if the storyteller does his job well, we fall in love with him; thus our Emotion Curve swings to very positive. But things can't stay that way for long. As conflict is established the audience senses danger and the Emotion Curve drops quickly. As the hero feels the negative vibe, so does the audience.

Now things slowly spiral out of control in a ever downward spin. There are moments when the curve comes up to the surface to catch its breath, but down it must go if the story is to be a success. Hollywood Script Doctor Bart Gavigan states it this way: ***"You must take the hero to the end of the line."*** We must drag him down to the depths of despair. The audience must sense his plight and realize disaster or death is but moments away.   This leads us to the single most important rule in telling blockbuster stories:

The End of the line!

55

The greater the distance between the Energy Curve and the Emotion curve at the Climax, the more rewarding and powerful the story.

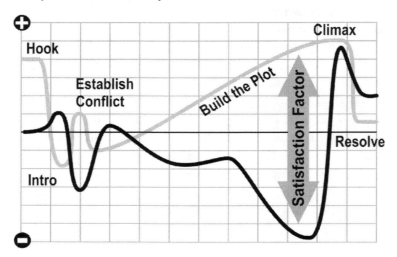

This is what is called the "satisfaction factor." Imagine our hero is a high school basketball player. He dreams of his small country high school winning the state championship. His teammates are all undersized but they make up for size with heart. There will be a lot of growth and many challenges to overcome in order to reach the state finals. Now, it has come down to one final game. Will the hero get what he wants?

In version 1, the team is really psyched up. They go out and in the first quarter run up a 30 point lead. They never look back but go on to easily win the state championship and the hero gets what he wants.

In version 2 the first quarter is tightly contested. It is only because of our hero's leadership that the team is able to stay within 3 points. But then it happens. One of the opposing players, the villain, intentionally elbows our hero in the ribs, sending him to the floor in extreme pain. A courtside physician declares that he has broken ribs and should sit out the rest of the game. His teammates fight valiantly, but without him on the court they are down by 12 at halftime. Things go from bad to worse in the third quarter, down by 23. He can't stand it anymore and has the doctor tape his ribs so he can play the fourth quarter. With our hero back on the court the team begins to play again and as the minutes tic by, the hero's team begins a comeback. It looks like it is going to be too little, too late. With only a minute on the clock they are down by 7. The villain is constantly throwing elbows at the hero. In spite of the opposition, the team manages to make up 4 of the points; but there are only 3 seconds left on the clock as the opposing team throws the ball into play. Our hero steals the ball and dribbles down the court, only to be met by the villain. The hero stops short of the three point line and as he goes up to shoot the villain smashes him in the ribs with a vicious forearm. The end of game siren blares as the ref's whistle blows and our hero crumples to the floor. The ball bangs against the rim, then off of the backboard, finally teetering on the rim. Ultimately it gives into gravity and falls through the hoop, tying up the game. The score is tied. Our hero is helped to his feet but he can't stand erect. He has been fouled and will get one additional shot. The game is tied, but it is obvious that he is through and without him on the court his team will lose in overtime. Slowly he hobbles to the foul line where the ref bounces the ball to him. This will be the last shot of regulation time. The villain is leering from one side of the court. He can taste the victory they will get in overtime. Our hero, unable to stand erect, bounces the ball a time or two and tries to pull the ball up into a shooting position, but the pain is two great. He looks at his teammates. There is such hope in their eyes but he is dizzy with pain. Then he has a flashback to his childhood and his dad teaching him in the backyard to shoot hoops. Closing his eyes, he bounces the ball three times and as the ball comes up to his hands on the third bounce, with one fluid motion, he guides the ball upward with an underhand motion. The entire crowd follows the ball upward as it rises in a lazy arc and slowly begins its descent. And then, without touching the rim, it falls through the net and his team has won the state championship!

Which story is more dramatic? **Take your hero to the end of the line.** In our basketball story the hero can barely standup let alone shoot a basket. But he overcomes insurmountable obstacles and challenges to get what he wants. That is the Satisfaction Factor.

Empathetic Devices

Great storytellers leverage empathetic devices to quickly bond their audience to the hero and to create tension with the villain.

How can we make the audience love our hero? What are some of the things that you love in other people? Loyalty, kindness, honesty, bravery, politeness, honor; well you get the idea. But we just can't come right out and say that our hero is a wonderful guy and wouldn't it be great to cheer for him the rest of the story? No, we must reveal his personality to the audience in such a way as to allow them to draw their own conclusions based upon the events of the story. There are a number of classic empathetic devices that are used over and over again. How many times have you heard of the weak nerd character trying to stop a bully from pounding someone weaker even than them? In one form or another this always plays well to the audience. They eat it up. Why? Because most of us were bullied at one time or another in our childhood or we saw someone else bullied and wish we had done something about it.

Everyone loves an underdog. Everyone roots for someone who has been wronged, wanting to have it made right. Characters who have lost parents or siblings immediately get the benefit of the doubt. Batman's parents murdered. Spiderman is an orphan whose uncle is murdered. Superman is orphaned and sent to earth. Indiana Jones suffers the death of his mother and is estranged from his father. In "Star Wars," Luke Skywalker is apparently an orphan and Princess Leia becomes an orphan.

People who are kind to animals are assumed to be good people. In this category, add people who animals are naturally drawn to, because this tells the audience that the guy must be okay because the dog likes him.

In one of the opening scenes of a Rambo movie a Vietnam war veteran is living on the streets. After just a few scenes he will be savaging the town, bringing vengeance down upon the bad guys, so it is pretty important for the writer to connect him to the audience real fast. Rambo sits down on the edge of the street with a sandwich in his hand. An old pitiful looking stray dog approaches him, begging. Rambo takes his own sandwich and feeds the dog. It is at that moment that the entire audience gives a collective sigh and accepts him as a good guy.

All villains should be hated, despised, and deserving of everything they get in the end. It is not only important that the audience is cheering for the hero, they must also be booing the villain. If the villain is too sympathetic there is the risk of the audience feeling sorry for him when he is defeated at the climax. The audience can actually turn on the hero and now you have a real mess on your hand. This is why Hollywood Blockbuster films usually have very very bad villains.

Villains often do something nefarious in their opening scene. This nefarious act is an empathetic device designed to make the audience hate or despise the villain. What might a villain do that is so heinous that no one can identify with them? Murdering an innocent person is popular. Murdering a child or a mother is even better, or worse, depending on how you look at it. Being rude, condescending, lying, or unfaithful are all good tools. In chick flicks the villain has almost always had sex with the heroine's best friend. There is no one perfect empathetic device applicable to every villain. Each story has its own needs and wants and the villain has to be treated in a realistic manner appropriate for the story. But, the storyteller must keep in mind the principle of discovering some empathetic device to ensure that the audience does not connect with the villain.

Analyzing a Bible Story

Our first step in understanding a Bible story is to read everything we can that relates to the story. In the case of "Jesus' baptism" through "Jesus' wilderness temptation" the story is told in Matthew, Mark, and Luke with additional insights in John. Each version is slightly different, but within the differences we find richness and detail.

1. Who is the Hero?

Jesus.

2. What does he want?

Jesus wants to be obedient to his Father, God. Matthew 3:15 says that Jesus went to the Jordan River to be baptized by John. Why did he do this? John also asked why, saying, "I have need to be baptized by you, and you come to me?" But Jesus is compelled to do the right thing. He answers that it is good to allow it, for the sake of doing all things right. This is what drives Jesus: doing that which is right, i.e. acting in obedience to his Father.

3. What is his wound?

Jesus is driven by an underlying wound. John 1:1-3 and Colossians 1:15,16 tells us that He is architect and creator of the universe and everything in it, including mankind. Jesus carries the wound that his creation has rejected the Father and has pursued Satan. This will weigh heavily upon his heart and color everything he does and says.

4. What is Jesus' weakness?

Is it even possible for Jesus to have a weakness? Does Jesus have a kryptonite? 2 Corinthians 13:4 alludes to his core weakness. Jesus is both 100% God, and 100% man (his weakness). Philippians 2:5-8 paints an interesting picture of Jesus' weakness.

> " *Have this attitude in yourselves which was also in Christ Jesus,* [6] *who, although He existed in the form of God, did not regard equality with God a thing to be grasped,* [7] *but emptied Himself, taking the form of a bond-servant, and being made in the likeness of men.* [8] *Being found in appearance as a man, He humbled Himself by becoming obedient to the point of death, even death on a cross.*"

As a human Jesus is plagued by all the temptations common to mankind including needing to eat, drink, and sleep. Jesus feels emotions like anger, joy, and sorrow. He became weary and finally he bled and died. Jesus, the creator of the universe chose to become weak for the sake of the wound.

5. The Villain

This is easy. Satan is the villain. Ok, we all agree he is the sum of all evil and that alone seems reason enough to explain why Satan will tempt Jesus. But that leaves us with a very shallow villain. What is his real motivation? Why does Satan so hate Jesus? Why is Satan trying to destroy him? Go back to the most embarrassing day in Satan's life, when according to Ezekiel 28:16 he was fired from his job as a cherubim in God's throne room, one who flew above the throne of God. Or more likely, trace back to a prophecy uttered by God himself in Genesis 3:15 where God said that one day a son of Eve's would crush Satan's head. Perhaps this prophecy had grown into a Satanic paranoia.

From this we began to understand the villain. Additionally this understanding allows us to add scripturally accurate color to our story.

6. What is the premise?

This is an intriguing part of storytelling preparation for every pastor /storyteller as we dig out the underlying truth that can guide our lives. Every story can contain multiple truths that can be drawn from it. This is one of the biggest risks that every story faces. Some storytellers are tempted to mix two or three truths together and in the end the audience usually goes away confused, with nothing.

Most Bible stories have a key verse or two, which when discovered, bring the story and the premise suddenly into context.

In Matthew 3:16 we find that Jesus first receives the Holy Spirit: " *After being baptized, Jesus came up immediately from the water; and behold, the heavens were opened, and he saw the Spirit of God descending as a dove and lighting on Him,"*

Then in Luke 4:1 we find that Jesus is full of the Spirit and being led by the Spirit: *"Jesus, full of the Holy Spirit, returned from the Jordan and was led around by the Spirit in the wilderness."*

Finally, in Luke 4:14 we find Jesus in the power of the Spirit: *"And Jesus returned to Galilee in the power of the Spirit"*

What can be drawn from these verses? In verse 1 Jesus is full of the Spirit and being led by the Spirit and then suddenly in verse 14 Jesus is full of the power of the Spirit! What happened between verse 1 and verse 14? The answer is obvious and simple. Jesus went through temptation and overcame Satan by the Word of God. What was it about this overcoming that made the difference in Jesus? The Bible says that Jesus is our example; thus he too had to be proved before he could be empowered. It is like the old gunsmiths who would double load a rifle barrel and fire it to prove that it could withstand the pressure and power of gunpowder.

This leads to our premise: ***Those whom God would use must first be tested and proved.***

7. The Setting

Our story begins at the Jordan River and then moves to the wilderness beyond Jordan. Although the Jordan valley is flat and green, to the east there are many barren hills with dry riverbeds. These dry river beds play a crucial role in part of the story. The Jordan River is fed all year round by the Sea of Galilee and a few other rivers. Seasonal rain runoff from all the surrounding countryside results in these dry river beds suddenly becoming rushing torrents, dragging sand and soil down to the Jordan and causing it to run brown. But the rushing water and soil slowly wear down the heavier softball size rocks smoothing them into round rocks about the same size, shape, and color of a typical Jewish loaf of bread. These bread-shaped rocks will be mentioned in Satan's first temptation of Christ.

Part of the setting requires understanding the cultural backdrop in which the story is told. Satan took Jesus to the top of the Temple and challenged him to throw himself off in order to reveal himself as Messiah to the Jewish Scribes and Pharisees below. It is important to understand that the Pharisees were the lawyers who studied the Old Testament and analyzed it down to the smallest detail. The Pharisees had to be convinced in some spectacular manner if they were ever to be convinced at all. Satan's use of Scripture was specifically designed to leverage this cultural dilemma that Jesus faced.

Assembling the Story

We have done a quick analysis of the story and its primary components, so now we must assemble the story according to our Hollywood Blockbuster method.

1. The Hook

The carpenter's work-bench was clean. No sawdust or wood shavings lay about the floor and all the tools that had faithfully served him were put away for the last time. The master carpenter and builder would never again return to his shop. Instead his footsteps led him from Nazareth in Galilee down to the Jordan River to a divine appointment with his cousin, John the Baptist.

We can only imagine what was going through Jesus' mind as he walked along. Most of the first 30 years of his life had been spent in Nazareth consumed with studying God's Word, praying, and making things out of wood. In many ways he was no different than any other young man of Nazareth. He knew that he had a unique relationship and calling with God; but his life had been simple without miracles or supernatural powers.

Now all of that was about to change.

2. The Introduction

In the life of a Jewis man, turning 30 years old is commonly accepted as the age at which a man can become a leader. For example, in Genesis 41:46, Joseph was 30 years old when he stood before Pharaoh and took over the responsibility of ruling Egypt. The Code of Jewish Law says a man should be at least 30 years old to serve as the cantor, to lead services during High Holy Days. Jesus is now 30. He is no longer perceived among his colleagues as just a young man, but now his fellow Jews can accept him as a leader.

John 1:38 tells us that John was baptizing near the village of Bethany, on the east side of the Jordan. Bethany lies at the mouth of a dry riverbed, called Wadi Kharrar, that normally only has water in it only during the rainy season. Wadi Kharrar is the place where the Prophet Elijah was taken up into heaven. 400 years later the Prophet Malachi would prophecy that Elijah would return before the Messiah would come. Now to the very place that Elijah ascended into heaven, we find the prophet who Jesus would equate to Elijah, baptizing and calling people to repentance.

3. Establishing the Conflict

Walking from Nazareth to Bethany would take Jesus almost a week. Each step of the over 80 mile journey brought him one step closer to his destiny. Scripture reveals what drove him onward. He wanted to obey his Father and fulfill God's plan for his life. Jesus knew from prophecy what was lying before him.

Jesus was not the only one who knew everything was about to change. Satan sensed his time to destroy his mortal enemy had come. A nagging fear plagued Satan ever since God had pronounced judgment upon Adam and Eve eons ago. God had promised that one of Eve's descendents would crush Satan's head. When Jesus was born Satan had tried to kill him by convincing King Herod to have all the babies in Bethlehem murdered. God warned Joseph in a dream and together with his parents, Jesus escaped to Egypt. Satan would be more subtle this time. For 30 years he had waited for this chance and he had carefully planned his attack.

4. Develop the Plot

When Jesus arrived at Bethany, John was baptizing people in a pool of water. Jesus descended into the water and approached his cousin.

John looked up at Jesus and suddenly recognized him. However, it wasn't his cousin Jesus that he saw, but someone much greater. In that moment, it was revealed to him who stood before him. Not a man. Not a relative. But the Christ. John had preached repentance for years. He had proclaimed that someone was coming who was greater than he. And now, standing before him, waiting to be baptized, was that very person.

John said, " I need to be baptized by You, and do You come to me?"

A more arrogant or self-driven man might have agreed with John and baptized him. But Jesus was not pursuing his own will, but rather the will of his Father.

"Let it be so now; it is proper for us to do this to fulfill all righteousness." Jesus said.

With that, the greater was baptized by the lesser. John lowered Jesus into the water and as Jesus came up, suddenly the heavens were opened. John saw the Spirit of God descending as a dove and landing on Jesus. Then a voice called out of the heavens saying, "This is My beloved Son, in whom I am well pleased!"

Jesus ascended out of the pool of water and climbed the hillside. 22 miles to the west lay Jerusalem and his destiny. But Jesus was full of the Spirit of God and was compelled by the Spirit to turn east toward the wasteland. And so, as Luke 4:1 says: " Jesus, full of the Holy Spirit, returned from the Jordan and was led around by the Spirit in the wilderness."

We can only imagine that this was not what Jesus had expected. Instead of beginning his ministry, the Spirit led him out to the wilderness where for 40 days he fasted. At the end of those days, Luke 4:2 says he became hungry. Everyone who has fasted more than a few days knows that somewhere around the third day your hunger leaves you. You can continue going without food and not be in any danger of starvation for many days. But when your hunger returns, it is a sign you are beginning to starve to death. If you don't eat soon the body begins to shut down and soon you will die. Jesus reached this point. He was at his physically weakest moment.

Satan was waiting for this moment. He had heard God's proclamation that Jesus was his Beloved Son. It was like a gauntlet thrown down at his feet. It was game on and

Satan was ready. He would not be rash or foolish. Patience and precise attacks would achieve more than careless manipulation of his pawns.

Satan watched Jesus ascend up into the wilderness. But he was no fool. He sensed that Jesus was strong and ready for a fight. Satan knew there was a connection between a man's physical strength and his spiritual health. When one of these became weak it usually affected the other. For 40 days Satan dogged Jesus' path, patiently waiting for the most opportune moment to attack. He had watched men starve to death before and after 40 days, he recognized the symptoms in Jesus. It was time to strike!

Jesus had walked along the dry riverbed of the wadi. He was feeling very weak and he sat down to rest for a moment. Suddenly he found that he was no longer alone. There standing before him was Satan. The two of them locked eyes for a moment. Jesus was tempted to just rebuke Satan and be done with him. But the Spirit of God inside him restrained him. He would not lash out of his own will, but would be led by God and Him only.

Satan squatted down in the dry riverbed and picked up a round river rock. The rock was worn smooth by the countless spring rains that filled the wadi when the water rushed down towards the Jordan. Subtle shades of brown speckled its surface. Satan looked into the eyes of Jesus and offered him the rock saying, "If you are the Son of God, tell this stone to become bread."

Jesus glanced down at the smooth rock. It looked exactly like one of the fresh baked loaves of bread that could be purchased in any village of Israel. His stomach rumbled at the thought. He knew he had the power of the Spirit to do such a thing. He also knew he had authority as the Son of God to turn the stone into bread. But he chose to submit to the authority of the Father. He would be only led by the Spirit, not by his human flesh.

Jesus looked from the stone into the eyes of Satan and said, "It is written, man shall not live on bread alone.'"

A sudden look of disappointment crossed Satan's face as he stood and tossed the rock back onto the riverbed. Looking toward the wall along the wadi he turned to Jesus and with a twist of his head invited the Christ to follow up the embankment.

Jesus sat for a moment not wanting to follow Satan anywhere, but the Spirit compelled him to follow. Jesus pulled himself up the rocky embankment to stand beside his enemy.

Satan stood looking off into the distance. He knew the Bible better than any Jewish Rabbi, Pharisee, or Scribe. It was clearly promised that the Messiah would one day rule over all the earth. But for the Messiah to get there would not be easy or pretty. Jesus topped the ridge and went over to stand beside Satan. Satan turned to Jesus and in one moment revealed to him all the kingdoms of the world.

"I will give You all this domain and its glory; for it has been handed over to me, and I give it to whomever I wish." Satan said. "Therefore if You worship before me, it shall all be Yours."

Jesus also knew the Bible. The prophecies concerning the Messiah were firmly committed to his memory. He knew there were two sets of prophecies. One set spoke of the glorious days when the Messiah would sit upon his throne and rule over all the earth. But there was another set of prophecies that were dark and painful. The Messiah would first be the suffering servant. The words of Isaiah the prophet, chapter 53; 3-5 haunted him:

" He was despised and forsaken of men,
A man of sorrows and acquainted with grief;
And like one from whom men hide their face
He was despised, and we did not esteem Him.
4 Surely our grief He Himself bore,
And our sorrows He carried;
Yet we ourselves esteemed Him stricken,
Smitten of God, and afflicted.
5 But He was pierced through for our transgressions,
He was crushed for our iniquities;
The chastening for our well-being *fell* upon Him,
And by His scourging we are healed."

Jesus understood what Satan was offering him. A short cut. Skip the suffering servant and move right on to ruling over the earth. But taking the short cut, the easy way out, would come with a price. He would have to reject the Lordship of his Father and submit himself to Satan. Jesus turned and faced Satan and said, "It is written, 'YOU SHALL WORSHIP THE LORD YOUR GOD AND SERVE HIM ONLY.'"

5. The Climax

Then Satan led Jesus to Jerusalem to stand on the pinnacle of the Temple. This would be Satan's most subtle attack. He would inspire Jesus to accomplish the prophecies with no strings attached.

Hundreds and hundreds of people could be seen in the Temple courtyards below. Pharisees and Sadducees were in the crowd and the High Priest was also there. All the people who needed to recognize him as God's Messiah were in the courtyard below him. Jesus knew most of them would never accept him and their rejection of him would lead to suffering. And Satan knew this as well.

"If You are the Son of God, throw Yourself down from here; for it is written, 'HE WILL COMMAND HIS ANGELS CONCERNING YOU TO GUARD YOU,' and, 'ON *their* HANDS THEY WILL BEAR YOU UP, SO THAT YOU WILL NOT STRIKE YOUR FOOT AGAINST A STONE.'" Satan said this in an attempt to appeal to Jesus' pride.

Jesus clearly knew what Satan was asking him to do. This temptation was appealing on so many levels. It appealed to the universal human need for acceptance from one's peers. It appealed to the basic self-preservation instinct. It also appealed to his pride. If he did this one thing, he would not have to deal with all the naysayers and critics. As he fell from the temple, the sudden appearance of angels would proclaim loud and clear that he was the Messiah. The leaders of Israel would fall in behind him and the entire nation would accept him. Satan was appealing to his human pride and offering him another short cut. But if he did this, he would not be in submission to the Father or the Father's will. This was not what Jesus wanted and so he answered Satan, "It is said, 'YOU SHALL NOT PUT THE LORD YOUR GOD TO THE TEST.'"

6. The Resolve

Suddenly Satan was gone and Jesus was back in the wilderness alone. He knew Satan would be back, but he also knew he had resisted the three great temptations of life: the lust of the flesh, the lust of the eye, and the pride of life.

Jesus turned toward Galilee. He would return there, there but things would be much different. For the man who went down to be baptized by John; the man upon whom the Holy Spirit had descended upon and then was led into the wilderness; the man Jesus Christ would return to the Galilee in the power of the Holy Spirit.

Storytelling Techniques

A well- crafted story that follows the Hollywood Blockbuster principles, is only half the battle. A story is nothing more than words on a page until it is told to an audience. Creating the story is a definite art form; telling the story is the other side of the same coin.

Some people are natural storytellers. They instinctively feel the ebb and flow of the energy of the story while subconsciously 'reading' their audience. The good news is that even if you are not a natural storyteller you can learn some techniques to enable you to 'deliver the goods.'

Voice inflection

As every public speaker knows, you can't stand up in front of an audience and talk in a monotone. But storytelling is much more dynamic than just giving a speech or preaching a sermon. The voice of the storyteller should follow the energy curve. The hook can be very intense with quick percussive sentences that segue into the more conversational tone of the introduction. Typically, as the energy rises sentences shorten and are spoken more quickly. This is especially important if there is a lot of action in your story. 'Spit it out, already.' No one wants to wait and hear flowery descriptions. The action is fast and furious and so should the storytelling.

Some stories are suspenseful at the climax. Energy can be very high while the action is extremely slow and almost incremental. Sentences typically will still be short, but not necessarily spoken rapidly.

Voice dynamics

As with inflection the voice should vary in loudness during the story. Hooks typically are louder and more demonstrative than the introduction. Sometimes the conflict is established loudly, other times softly and sinisterly. The key is to make the voice fit the action as it is occurring.

Humor

Some stories are humorous. Some genres need a little humor to release tension. Action adventure movies often intersperse moments of comedy to allow the audience to release the building tension. An audience member has only so much adrenaline. If the story has too much energy and intensity at the beginning, the audience can be exhausted before the climax. A momentary spark of humor releases the tension and allows the audience to build toward the climax.

Humor can also be used when telling a story that the audience probably already knows. Certain Bible stories like David and Goliath are known even outside of Christian circles. Thus the audience might be tempted to tune out the storyteller. Adding humor to a familiar story can breathe life into it and keep the audience engaged.

One of the easiest methods of adding humor is to use a modern juxtaposition to a story that took place in the past. For example:

"Revelation tells us that Satan is the accuser of the brethren and he stands before the throne of God day and night accusing us of our sins.

Now back on earth, Jesus went about the countryside healing the sick and casting out demons. This was a real problem for Satan because it was impacting his evil work on earth. But Jesus was only one person, in one place, at one time. How much trouble could he possibly cause? He was nothing more than a nuisance , a brush fire.

But then Jesus gathered all of his disciples around him. He gave them authority over the demonic spirits and sent them out across Israel. Suddenly what started as a brush fire was roaring into a wild fire, sweeping across the country.

Meanwhile, Satan was before the throne, just beginning to start up a fresh batch of complaining and accusing, when suddenly his cell phone rang. "Uh, excuse me God, I, uh, need to take this." Satan said, as he put the phone to his ear. "Slow down. What's that? You got cast out? You're where? Well stay away from the pigs." Satan hung up his phone and spun around to face God. "Ah, sorry about that. Now where was I?" Suddenly Satan's phone rang again. "Excuse me again. What is it? Healing? Where? One minute, let me put you on hold. Yeah? You got cast out too? All right, all right. I guess this Jesus and his disciples are out of control! If I want something done right, then I'll have to do it myself!" And with that Satan stormed out of God's throne room and raced to the earth. He would deal with Jesus once and for all. Indeed he would set a plan into action. He would possess Judas, and then use Judas to betray Jesus to the High Priest of the Jews."

Well, as you can see, you can have a little fun with a story. There are some simple guidelines to remember if you do this with a Bible story. First, make sure the embellishment is so crazy that no one would believe it actually happened that way. Second, make sure the embellishment stays true to the principles of Scripture. As a general rule, I never put words into Jesus' mouth. If I say Jesus said something, you will usually find those very words in the Scripture.

Body Language

Storytelling can be a real workout. I tell the story of the little boy giving his lunch to Jesus to feed the 5000. When it comes to for the part where Andrew brings the boy to Christ, I typically walk a few steps to one side and act as if I am coaxing the boy to go to Jesus. Then I play the role of the boy, holding the basket in his hands, he walks hesitantly toward Jesus. When it is time for the boy to give the basket to Jesus, I have a little

78

exaggerated fun. I clutch the invisible basket tightly to my chest as I first look up to where Jesus would be standing and then back toward Andrew, shaking my head as if to say no, "my basket." Finally, I bow my head and lift the invisible basket up, just as a little child might. Now all this acting happens while I am telling the story. The physicality adds a layer of visual communication that combined with telling the story, is powerful indeed. When the physicality is combined with humor, you create a memorable mental image.

Audience engagement

Storytellers often forget that the audience can become part of the story. This is accomplished as easily as merely asking the audience a question and encouraging them to answer. In the illustration we used before of Satan standing before the throne of God, we can make a subtle change that will allow us to engage the audience.

"Satan slammed his cell phone shut and stormed out of the throne room of God. He was in a rage. His demons could not control Jesus or his disciple. Well, he thought, if you want something done right, then you . . . " (Allow the audience to verbally fill in the blank.)

Something as simple as the example above is extremely powerful to keep your audience engaged. In addition, it burns the concept into their minds. A person can see something and not remember it. He can hear something and not remember it. He can actually see and hear something and he just might remember it. But when a person sees, hears, and then engages his mind to reach and state a conclusion -- then suddenly he has internalized the concept.

Props

I love props. **An attention grabbing object I can hold in my hand is a powerful tool.** When I tell the story of Jael I hold a wooden tent peg loosely in my hand as I describe Jael placing the peg against the head of General Sisera. Then, taking a wood mallet, I smack the top of the tent peg as I tell how Jael drove the peg through the general's head and into the sand. The loud bang of the mallet upon the peg and the peg sliding down through my hand has a powerful auditory and visual effect. It often causes the audience to wince as they mentally complete the picture of the peg going through a skull.

Read Your Audience

Every storyteller must learn to read his/her audience. Sometimes your audience is eating out of your hand and you can embellish your story to great effect. At other times an audience may be in a hurry for you to finish so they can rush out the door and beat the other churches to the favorite local restaurant. In that situation, to continue or expand a story is a disaster.

There are some fairly obvious visual clues to help in reading your audience.

1. Where are they looking?

If your audience is looking directly at you, then you probably have them engaged. But if they are looking at their watches, each other, or (the ultimate sign that you have lost them!) if they are looking at their phones; then it is time to wrap it up and move on.

2. What are they doing?

Are they leaning forward with their eyes on you? It tells you they are in the palms of your hands. If they are leaning back, fidgeting, and (heaven help you!) whispering; you might have completely lost them.

3. How are they reacting?

What are the faces of your audience saying? Many people are an open book to be read by all. Are they smiling and laughing at the humorous parts? Are they watching intensely when you come to a dramatic part? Or, do they have a blank look on their face? Are their faces telling you they are not getting it?

Hollywood Blockbuster Sermons

Introduction, three points, an illustration, and a closing. These are the things we learned in Bible college. Of course, it's a lot more complex than that. Indeed, it *is* a lot more complex than that. And that really is the point. We often create sermons that only a small portion of the congregation is equipped to totally understand and take away with them. This chapter introduces a different method of looking at sermons and building effective and memorable messages.

Understand your audience.

- 6 out of 10 people in your audience are visual learners.
- 3 out of 10 people in your audience are oral learners.
- 1 out of 10 people in your audience are either kinesthetic /tactile learners or read/write learners.

Now most people are not exclusively one learning style, but often are a combination of two or even three methods. However, most people have one dominate method of learning that they subconsciously prefer.

While our DNA might predetermine our learning style education, especially higher education, will greatly influence how we think and process information. Higher critical thinking is something we are not born with, but learn in college.

- 2 out of 10 people in your audience will have a college degree.
- 2 out of 10 people in your audience attended some college but never earned a degree.
- 6 out 10 people in your audience never attended college.

This statistics give us insight into what percentage of the general population might operate in a higher critical thinking mode. Why is this important? While in Bible College I was taught "higher critical thinking." At least this was the goal of my professors. We were taught

Homiletics, Hermeneutics, various theories of this, that, and whatever. All critically analyzed and postulated by numerous great thinkers of the past 2000 years of church history. This education has proven a tremendous blessing to me over my 30 years of ministry and I will be forever grateful for my talented and brilliant instructors. Whereas higher critical thinking equipped me to analyze and understand the Bible, it did not prepare me to effectively communicate to the average person in my congregation who was not trained to think similarly.

The education statistics above would lead us to assume that we might have 2 out of 10 people in our congregation who are 'higher critical' thinkers. If we combine the education statistics with the learning style statistics we can draw a simple profile of the average person sitting in your audience:

A visual/oral learner with little or no college education.

Why is this important? Almost all people are genetically predisposed to oral storying as a primary communication method. Western civilization and higher education have placed a layer of critical thinking and analysis over the top of this genetic predisposition. Typically the less education a person has, the more likely he or she is to be more heavily wired and more easily captivated with stories. Thus, a more complete profile of the typical person sitting in the audience would be:

A visual/oral learner with little or no college education who prefers stories to logical arguments.

Knowing this could potentially skew everything we do in the pulpit if we desire to be effective to the greatest percentage of our audience. But we don't want to throw the "baby out with the bathwater." Although standing in front of your congregation and telling 30 minutes of stories might make you popular with part of the congregation, it would leave 30-40% of the congregation wanting something more.

A hybrid approach, relying heavily on storying and including powerful Scriptural principles and insights, will effectively communicate with the broadest audience.

There is a trend developing among a group of pastors who are experiencing rapid growth in their churches. They have developed a one point sermon style based heavily upon storytelling. This seems shallow at first especially since when we compare this simple approach to our well developed multi-point messages. But they are operating on a very simple principle. It is better for a person to leave a service with a clear understanding of one powerful principle than to leave feeling that they had been told many important things but having a hard time remembering any one of them.

Let's look at a sermon from the Hollywood Blockbuster perspective: Hook, Introduction, Conflict, Build the Principle, Climax, and Resolve (the Appeal).

Let's keep in mind our audience profile: Visual/Oral learners.   We can't just stalk and talk and talk. Remember only 3 in 10 people are oral learners.   We must include occasional visuals to keep everyone engaged. Powerful visuals will burn your message into their minds for the rest of their lives.

Here are two examples of story driven sermons. The first is unique in that the entire sermon is stories. The second example is a hybrid sermon mixing traditional style along with the story of Jesus' baptism.

Example 1:

What is in your hand?

INTRODUCTION:

My wife and I are celebrating our thirtieth wedding anniversary this year. I have to admit, it almost didn't happen. Like most young men, I fell deeply in love and decided that I desperately wanted Rhonda to be my wife. Now most women do not realize this, but when young men fall in love they can be incredibly romantic. Thus, I wanted to propose to Rhonda in a romantic way. Years earlier I sold a van and suddenly found myself with a few thousand dollars profit. It must have been the Spirit of the Lord that inspired me to take some of the money and purchase an unset diamond. Now I had found the love of my life and it was time to get the diamond set. Although I had been promised the completed ring on a certain date, the jeweler got behind schedule and the ring would not be ready until the morning of my big plans. To make matters worse, as I was walking out the door to pick Rhonda up and take her to Disney World for the big proposal, my pastor called and offered me a mission trip to Panama. Before it was all said and done, I was almost an hour late picking Rhonda up. You can imagine the icy reception I received. Now I needed to pick up the ring from the jeweler without letting Rhonda know what I was up too. Being the incredibly sneaky and stupid male that I am, I parked Rhonda in an alley behind the jeweler, next to a dumpster. If she was icy when I picked up her, she was absolutely frozen when I got back into the car. We didn't talk much on the way to Disney as we were now almost 2 hours behind schedule.

What is the most romantic location in Disney World? Cinderella's castle! You've got it. And on the second floor of the castle is St. Stephen's restaurant. So, since it was near lunchtime, I made reservations, and soon we found ourselves sitting at a very small table in the middle of the restaurant. Carefully I slid the ring box out of my pocket and set it on my lap.

Then, looking into her beautiful eyes, I said, "Rhonda, I love you."

"Really? How much?" she asked.

"Enough to ask you to marry me." I said with a silly grin.

"Are you serious?" She asked somewhat confused.

"This serious!" And I pulled the ring box out and set it in front of her. It was a priceless moment as she looked first at the ring, then at me, then at the ring, then back at me, unable to speak.

It was the first and only time in thirty years of marriage that Rhonda was speechless! I came with a ring in hand and got the bride of my dreams.

About the same time thirty years ago another young women was married. Since I am not sure how to spell or pronounce her Maasai name, we will call her Esther. The Maasai are a primitive people who herd cattle and worship spirits in rocks and animals. Esther was born and raised in a mud hut with a thatch roof in northern Tanzania. She was just three years old when a Maasai Elder visited her father and gave him two cows. She didn't know it, but she had just become engaged. Each year for the next ten years the same man visited her father with a war club in one hand and halter ropes around the necks of two cows in the other hand.

Esther was just thirteen years old when the man arrived for the last time. Her father called her and put her hand in the hand of the stranger. Then her mother snapped a flat disc of beads around her neck, and in that moment, she was married. Suddenly she was dragged away from her mother, her home, and everything she had ever known. She was now married and if she did not do everything her husband demanded of her, she would be beaten.

Two true stories of marriage. Each suitor came with something in his hands; I came with a ring, the other came with a war club.

1. The value of what we hold in our hands is irrelevant when given to God.

Exodus chapter 3 tells about a man named Moses and his encounter with God. Moses was eighty years old and living in the desert shepherding a flock of sheep. He once was the adopted grandson of the Pharaoh of Egypt. But in an angry rage he murdered an Egyptian task-master who he saw cruelly beating his fellow Hebrews.

When word got out about his crime, he fled Egypt into the wilderness. There, in the land of Midian, he met a beautiful Kenite shepherd girl and started a new life.

That was forty years ago. Now, eighty years old, Moses was looking forward to retirement. One day Moses was out with his sheep when he saw an incredible sight; a bush that burned but was not consumed. Suddenly, out of the bush came a voice.

"Moses!" Moses looked around in shock. "Moses! Take off your sandals for you are standing on holy ground!" the voice said.

Moses kicked off his sandals and stood clutching his shepherd's staff. "Moses, I want you to go to Egypt and tell Pharaoh to let my people go."

Now Moses was terrified. "Uh, God. Like, who is going to believe me? I'm a shepherd and I stink like sheep!"

God replied, "What is in your hand, Moses?"

"Uh, this? Ummm. A stick?"

"Throw down your stick, Moses!" God commanded.

Now Moses suddenly got real possessive of his stick and he clutched it tightly against his chest and murmured, "My stick."

"Moses! Throw your stick down!" God commanded again.

Then Moses threw down his shepherd's staff and it became a snake. "Snake!" He cried as he fled from it.

But God was not through with Moses. "Pick up the snake, Moses. Not by that end, do you want to get bit? Grab it by the other end." So Moses grabbed the snake by the tail it became a staff again.

Thus Moses, with nothing more than a stick, actually a shepherd's staff, went to Egypt and delivered 3 million Jews from Egyptian bondage.

As long as the stick was in Moses' hands, it was just a stick! But, when Moses gave his stick to God it became an instrument in the hand of God, able to perform incredible miracles.

2. God is not a respecter of any person - Male or female. God is merely looking for people who are willing to give, to let go. Judges chapter 4 tells this story.

400 years later one of Moses' distant relatives would follow in his footsteps. Heber, the Kenite, was a Bedouin. Heber decided to leave the land of Midian and pitch his tent near the town of Kedesh. It was a long hard walk but the hillsides were filled with great places to graze his sheep. The Israelites were peaceful and the Canaanite King, Jabin, had made a peace treaty with him so he would be protected from the raids of Sisera the Canaanite general. Now, under the massive branches of

an oak tree, he called his wife and children together to pitch their tent and to make camp.

His wife, Jael, along with her daughters, spread the tent out and began to hammer pegs into the ground to hold the tent ropes. Then, as Heber sang, the tent was lifted into the air on four stout poles. Jael and her daughters worked to pound more pegs into the ground. All was good. This is what Jael desperately wanted, a safe place to raise her children. A place with plenty of pasture for the sheep and fresh water to drink.

Jabin, the King of the Canaanites, had oppressed the Israelites for years. His brilliant general, Sisera, would ride out of their castle fortress with 800 chariots of iron and steal the harvest from the Israelites.

Now the Israelites cried out to God because the oppression was so great. And God answered by speaking through the prophetess Deborah. She called Barack and gave him the word from God. "Barack, gather up an army of 10,000 and go to the river Kishon where God will deliver General Sisera into your hand."

Apparently Barack did not like being told what to do by a woman -- especially when the woman him to go to war. After all, he would risk his skin while she stayed home watching TV and eating bon-bons. "I'll go if you go!" Barack challenged her, figuring this would be the end of this crazy talk about going to war. But Deborah called his bluff, saying she would go with him, but with one caveat. "The honor shall not be yours on the journey that you are about to take, for the LORD will sell Sisera into the hands of a woman."

So Deborah, Barack and 10,000 of their friends, armed with spears, swords, pruning hooks and other garden implements, set off to do battle with Sisera.

When General Sisera heard the Jews had come out to do battle, he gathered his army along with his 800 iron chariots and went out for what he thought would be a great and glorious day of victory. He would rout the Jews, steal the gold and silver off their dead bodies, and then follow up with another romp through the northern tribes to steal everything that was not bolted down.

Things did not go well for General Sisera. God was with the Israelites and they thoroughly thumped his army, routing them. This had never happened before. The last thing Sisera wanted was to be captured by a bunch of angry farmers so he leaped off of his chariot and made a bee line back to the castle at Hazor. But he wasn't alone. The Jews saw him flee and they were now in hot pursuit.

You might wonder why it was such a big deal to capture this one man. In these times most armies were made up of farmers, villains, and thugs. But "generals" were those trained in warfare. A good general could raise up an army from among the countryside and win victories. Destroying General Sisera's army only delayed the next attack. The Israelites must kill the head of the snake to truly be free from his oppression.

Sisera ran for his life. He could hear the Israelites in the distance pursuing him. He searched for a place to hide because he was still many miles from Hazor. As he crossed over a small ridge, there before him was the camp of Heber the Kenite. An ally! Surely they would hide him. Down into the camp he raced. But Heber and the all the other men were gone. They were somewhere in the nearby hills watching their flocks of sheep. But standing outside of the Bedouin's tent was a beautiful young woman, Heber's wife, Jael.

Jael knew at once who this was in her encampment. She had seen General Sisera before and there was no mistaking his ornate and expensive armor. Now, this one man alone in their camp, risked destroying everything she wanted. She knew none of the men of her family were near and whatever was to be done, she would have to do. "Don't run any further. You'll be okay here," she said.

Sisera was exhausted. This was exactly what he needed. Without asking, he walked into her tent and collapsed on the floor. "Give me something to drink," he gasped as the exhaustion overcame him. Jael gave him a skin of milk to drink and covered him with one of her hand made carpets. "Stand in the doorway of the tent," he ordered. "And if anyone comes near tell them that the tent is empty." Jael immediately went and stood at the entrance to the tent. Within a few minutes Sisera fell into a deep sleep and began snoring.

Now Jael had a problem. What happened in the next few minutes potentially could destroy everything she wanted. First, she had a man in her tent. That was equivalent to adultery among the Bedouin. Second, she heard the approaching Israelite search party. If they found Sisera hiding in her tent they would not only kill Sisera, but they might kill her and her entire family for sheltering him! But what could she do? She was just a young woman. She had no sword or spear and even if she had, she did not know how to use them. She was not a warrior. She was just a Bedouin girl and General Sisera was a seasoned warrior, clad in armor. At the most, she might strike one blow. If it did not kill him, he would rise up and kill her, then her children. Out of the corner of her eye, lying along the edge of the tent, she spotted something with which she was very familiar, a tent peg and a large wooden mallet. Leaning over she quietly picked up the hammer and peg. Taking a deep breath to steady her nerves, she quietly stepped into her tent and knelt alongside the sleeping general. Very carefully she laid the tent peg against the general's head and then, with one well-practiced blow, drove the tent peg through his head and into the ground.

That day God delivered all of Israel from the oppression of the Canaanites -- through a sharpened stick held in the hands of a young Bedouin woman.

3. God does not care how old you are. He looks for people who are willing to give him what they hold in their hands.

Just down the road from where Jael won her great victory lies the Sea of Galilee. The Sea of Galilee is really just a small lake, about 7- 8 miles wide and 13 miles long. On the northwest bank is the fishing village of Capernaum, where Jesus used a house as his base of operation. The house was in constant commotion with people coming and going as Jesus healed the sick and ministered to the needy.

About 8 miles down the coast was the city of Tiberius, built by King Herod to be his royal city. Herod had married the divorced wife of his brother, which was against Jewish law. This of course could not go without comment from John the Baptist, after which he found himself arrested and sitting in Herod's dungeon. So, while Jesus was ministering up the road in Capernaum, Herod was partying with his buds down in Tiberius. At the peak of the party, Herod's step-daughter danced for everyone and Herod offered her a reward. It was common for great people to offer as much as half of their kingdom as a reward to express how pleased they felt. However, no one ever took them up on it. But Herod's step-daughter talked to her mother who hated John the Baptist, and asked that Herod give her the head of John the Baptist on a plate. Not wanting to go back on an offer made in front of his guests, Herod sent to the dungeon and commanded that John was beheaded.

When the disciples of John heard about this, they came and claimed his body so they could properly bury it. Then, in great sorrow, they plodded up the road to Capernaum to tell Jesus.

Into the commotion of Jesus' house came the mourning disciples of John. Jesus was shocked at the news. First, John was his own cousin. But also because Jesus understood that with John' death, the last of the prophets of the Old Covenant were gone. Jesus was deeply moved and suddenly the chaos swirling around him was too much.

"Peter! Get the boat ready. I want to go to the other side of the sea to the wilderness where I can spend some quiet time with God," Jesus said.

Within a few minutes all the disciples and Jesus left the house and walked to the water's edge, climbed into the boat and pushed off into the sea. The boat was not very large, perhaps 8 feet wide and 30 feet long. Four of the disciples manned the oars while Peter set the sail and

John stood at the tiller. It would only be about a seven mile journey across the northern end of the Sea of Galilee, with the boat never more than a few miles off shore.

But Jesus and his disciples would not make a clean escape. People from the village saw them get into the boat and begin to row to the opposite shore. It didn't take long for a small mob to form as people hurried along the shore of the Sea of Galilee following the progress of Jesus and the disciples. As the crowd grew, people from the surrounding villages came down and after discovering where the mob was going, they joined in. The crowd walked for a few hours and it became obvious where Jesus and the Disciples would come ashore.

Jesus could see the crowd growing larger and larger. His plans for a quick get-away were spoiled and now thousands of people awaited him in the wilderness on the eastern shore of the Sea of Galilee. His 'alone time' with God would have to wait. He and his disciples came ashore and soon he was healing the sick and teaching the crowd. By now the sun was well past noon and was beginning its descent.

"The people have been with us all day without food," he said to his disciples. "Give them something to eat."

The disciples looked at each in shock. They had left so quickly that none of them had thought to bring food. That, however, was the least of their worries. "Master, we have no food. And even if there was a place to buy bread, it would take almost $25,000 to buy enough so that everyone just had a small piece," one disciple said. "Send them home to their villages," another disciple added.

"No, I want you to feed them, "Jesus insisted.

The disciples just looked at one another in shock and disbelief. Then Andrew stepped forward pushing a little boy who was carrying a lunch basket. "Go ahead, give it to Jesus," Andrew encouraged. The little boy clutched tightly to his basket, after all, it was his lunch. You can almost hear what must be going through the child's mind, 'Mine! My lunch!' But looking first at Jesus, then at his lunch, then back to Jesus, the boy's face brightened and he smiled as he gave his lunch to the Lord.

Jesus opened the basket. There were five small dinner rolls and two little salted fish, fins and all. After blessing the lunch, he gave it to the disciples and with it, they fed 5,000 men plus women and children.

As long as the lunch was in the hands of the child it was nothing more than lunch. But when given to the Lord it was multiplied beyond belief and thousands of people were fed.

4. God does not care who you are: boy, girl, old, young, shepherd, or housewife. God asks everyone of us the same question, "What is in your hand?"

In each of these stories, what they held in their hands was commonplace. A shepherd and his staff. A Bedouin and her tent peg. A child and his lunch.

Everyone of us holds something in our hands that seem insignificant and unimportant. Yet, if we are sensitive to the Holy Spirit and open to the voice of God, we might hear him saying, "What do you have in your hand? Will you give it to me?"

Example 2: A hybrid message

This message is a hybrid message using a strong visual coupled with a powerful story. This sermon is based on the story of Jesus and his temptation in the wilderness.

Please note that this message was originally preached in the early 1990's before gun violence became such a hot topic. Something else to keep in mind this sermon was delivered in Florida where gun control laws are much different than in some northern states. Although this sermon would not be used today it is a good example of a message targeting an specific audience for a specific time.

God's Formula for Spiritual Power

1. The Hook

Have you wished you had the supernatural power that Peter or John displayed in the New Testament? Wouldn't it be awesome to heal the sick or perform other great miracles? Why do we see so little of God's miraculous power at work in our church today?

I have something in this bag *(holding up the bag)* that will help us understand a very simple and basic principle of God and his supernatural power. *(Open bag and hold up handgun. There typically is a gasp from the audience!)*

This Colt Combat Commander is a powerful weapon. Now, I need someone to hold this gun until later in the sermon when I need it. Who would like to keep this safe until it is needed? *(A few hands typically go up and the stress level with the audience goes up as well.)* There in the front row is a little boy. He looks like he would love to hold this for me. *(The audience suddenly becomes vocal saying no!)* Obviously we don't want this kind of power in the hands of a seven year old. Do we have a law enforcement officer in the room? *(Prearranged officer comes to the front, the gun is placed back in the bag, and then handed over to the officer.)* Does everyone feel better now? *(Obvious sighs of relief in the room.)*

2. The Introduction

Why do we feel better? The answer is obvious. The police officer has been trained to handle weapons. He has been proven to be reliable and trustworthy. The child, on the other hand, is an unknown. He is probably immature. We don't trust his wisdom or understanding of the potential harm he could inflict with such a powerful weapon.

What about the supernatural power of God? Is it something that should be in the hands of immature and unproven Christians?

3. Establish the Conflict

This is the conflict that rages within each of us.

John 14:12
Truly, truly, I say to you, he who believes in Me.
the **works** that I do, he will do also;
and **greater works** than these he will do; because I go to the Father.

But where are the works? Where are the miracles? Is it because we don't believe enough? Why?

God has a simple formula for the supernatural endowment of power in the life of the believer.

Be filled + Be led + Be proven = Dunamis (Power)

We find the perfect example of this in the life of Christ.

4. Build (The Story)

The carpenter's work-bench was clean. No sawdust or wood shavings lay about the floor. All the tools that had faithfully served him had been put away for the last time. The master carpenter and builder would never again return to his shop. Instead his footsteps led him from Nazareth in Galilee down to the Jordan River. He had a divine appointment with his cousin, John the Baptist.

Imagine what was going through Jesus' mind as he walked along the Jordan. Most of the first 30 years of his life had been spent in Nazareth consumed with studying God's Word, praying, and building things made of wood. In many ways he was no different than any other young man of Nazareth. He knew he had a unique relationship and calling with God. But his life had thus far been simple without miracles or supernatural powers.

But all of that was about to change.

Turning 30 years old is significant in the lives of Jewish men. It is widely accepted as the age at which a man can become a leader. In Genesis 41:46 Joseph was 30 years old when he stood before Pharaoh and took over the responsibility of ruling Egypt. The Code of Jewish Law requires a man to be at least 30 years old to serve as the cantor to lead services during High Holy days in the synagogue. Jesus is now 30. He is no longer to be perceived as a young man, but now is acceptable among his fellow Jews as a leader.

In John 1:38 we find that John was baptizing near a village called Bethany. Bethany is located at the mouth of Wadi Kharrar, a dry riverbed that normally has water in it only during the rainy season. Wadi Kharrar is famous as the place where the Prophet Elijah was taken up into heaven. 400 years later the Prophet Malachi would prophecy that Elijah would return before the Messiah would come. Now to the very place that Elijah ascended into heaven, we find the prophet who Jesus would equate to Elijah, baptizing and calling people to repentance.

Walking from Nazareth to Wadi Kharrar would take Jesus almost a week. Each step of the more than 80 mile trip brought him one step closer to his destiny. Scripture reveals what drove him. He wanted to obey his Father and fulfill God's plan for his life. Jesus knew from prophecy what was lying before him and each step drew him closer.

Jesus was not the only one who knew that everything was about to change. Satan sensed his time to destroy his mortal enemy had come as well. A nagging fear plagued him since God had pronounced judgment upon Adam and Eve eons ago. It had been promised that one of Eve's descendents would crush Satan's head. When

Jesus was born Satan had tried to kill him through the efforts of King Herod who decreed that all the babies of Bethlehem be murdered. But God warned Joseph in a dream and they escaped to Egypt. Satan would be more subtle this time. He had waited 30 years for this chance and had carefully been planning his attack.

When Jesus arrived at Wadi Kharrar John was down in a pool of water baptizing people. Jesus descended into the water and approached his cousin.

John looked up at Jesus and suddenly recognized him. But it wasn't his cousin Jesus that he saw, but something much greater. In that moment, into the mind of the prophet, was revealed who stood before him. Not a man. Not a relative. But the Christ. John had been preaching repentance for years. He had been proclaiming that one was coming whom was greater than he. And now, standing before him, waiting to be baptized, was that very man.

" I have need to be baptized by You, and yet You come to me?" John said.

A more arrogant or self-driven man might have agreed with John and baptized him. But Jesus was not pursuing his own will, but rather that of his Father. "Permit *it* at this time; for in this way it is fitting for us to fulfill all righteousness." Jesus said. And with that, the greater was baptized by the lesser. John lowered Jesus into the water and as he came up suddenly the heavens were opened and he saw the Spirit of God descending as a dove and landing upon him. Then a voice called out of the heavens saying, "This is My beloved Son, in whom I am well pleased!"

Jesus ascended out of the pool of water and climbed the hillside of the Wadi. 22 miles to the west lay Jerusalem and his destiny. But Jesus was full of the Spirit of God and was compelled by the Spirit to turn east towards the wastelands. And so, as Luke 4:1 says: " Jesus, full of the Holy Spirit, returned from the Jordan and was led around by the Spirit in the wilderness."

We can only imagine that this was not what Jesus had expected. Instead of beginning his ministry, the Spirit has led him out to the wilderness where for 40 days he has fasted. At the end of those days, Luke 4:2 says that he became hungry. Everyone who has ever fasted more than a few days knows that somewhere around the third day your hunger leaves you. You can continue going without food and not being in any danger of starvation for many days. But when your hunger returns it is a sign that your are beginning to starve to death. If you don't eat soon you body will begin to shut down and you will die. Jesus has reached this point. He is at his physically weakest point.

Satan has been waiting for this moment. He had heard God's proclamation that Jesus was his Son. It was like a gauntlet thrown down at his feet. It was game on and Satan was ready. He would not be rash or foolish this time. Patience and precise attacks would achieve more than careless manipulation of his pawns.

Satan had watched Jesus ascend up into the wilderness. But he was no fool. He sensed that Jesus was strong and ready for a fight. Satan knew that there was a connection between a man's physical strength and their spiritual health. When one became weak it usually affected the other. For 40 days Satan dogged Jesus' path patiently waiting for the most opportune moment to attack. He watched men starve to death before and now he recognized the symptoms in Jesus. It was time to strike!

Jesus had been walking along the dry riverbed of a wadi. He was feeling very weak. When he sat down to rest for a moment he suddenly found that he was no longer alone. There standing before him was Satan. The two of them locked eyes for a moment. They both knew who the other was. Jesus was tempted to just rebuke him and be done with him. But the Spirit inside him restrained him and he would not lash out of his own will, but would be led by God and him only.

Satan squatted down in the dry riverbed and picked up a round river rock. The rock was worn smooth by countless spring rains that had filled the wadi as the water rushed down towards the Jordan. Subtle shades of brown speckled its surface. Satan looked into the eyes of Jesus and offered him the rock saying, "If you are the Son of God, tell this stone to become bread."

Jesus glanced down at the smooth rock. It looked exactly like one of the fresh baked loaves of bread that could be purchased in any village of Israel. His stomach rumbled at the thought. He knew that he had the power of the Spirit to do such a thing. He also knew that he had the authority as the Son of God to turn the stone into bread. But he had chosen to submit himself to the authority of the Father. He would be only led by the Spirit, not by his human flesh.

Jesus looked from the stone up into the eyes of Satan and said, "It is written, 'Man shall not live on bread alone.'"

A sudden look of disappointment crossed Satan's face as he stood and tossed the rock back onto the riverbed. Looking towards the top of the wadi he turned to Jesus and with a twist of his head invited the Christ to follow up the embankment.

Jesus sat for a moment not wanting to follow Satan anywhere, but the Spirit compelled him to follow and Jesus pulled his way up the rocky embankment to stand beside his enemy.

Satan stood looking off into the distance. He knew the Bible better than any Jewish Rabbi, Pharisee, or Scribe. It was clearly promised the Messiah would someday rule over all the earth. Jesus topped the ridge and went over to stand beside him. Satan turned to Jesus and in one moment revealed to him all the kingdoms of the world.

"I will give You all this domain and its glory; for it has been handed over to me, and I give it to whomever I wish." Satan said. "Therefore if You worship before me, it shall all be Yours."

Jesus also knew the Bible. The reality of the prophecies concerning the Messiah had been committed to memory. He knew that there were two sets of prophecies. One set spoke all of the glorious days when the Messiah would sit upon his throne and rule over all the earth. But there was another set of prophecies that were dark and painful. The Messiah would first be the suffering servant. The words of Isaiah the prophet, chapter 53;3-5 haunted him, saying;

" He was despised and forsaken of men,
A man of sorrows and acquainted with grief;
And like one from whom men hide their face
He was despised, and we did not esteem Him.
⁴ Surely our grief He Himself bore,
And our sorrows He carried;
Yet we ourselves esteemed Him stricken,
Smitten of God, and afflicted.
⁵ But He was pierced through for our transgressions,
He was crushed for our iniquities;
The chastening for our well-being *fell* upon Him,
And by His scourging we are healed."

Jesus understood what Satan was offering him; a short cut. Skip the suffering servant and move right on to ruling over the earth. But it would come with a price. He would have to reject the Lordship of his Father and submit himself to Satan. Jesus turned and faced Satan as he said, "It is written, 'YOU SHALL WORSHIP THE LORD YOUR GOD AND SERVE HIM ONLY.'"

Satan then led Jesus to Jerusalem and had him stand on the pinnacle of the Temple. This would be his most subtle attack. He would inspire Jesus to accomplish that which the prophets had prophesied, without any strings attached.

Jesus could see hundreds and hundreds of people in the Temple courtyards bellow. Pharisees and Sadducees were intermixed in the crowd. The High Priest himself was also present. All the people who needed to recognize him as God's Messiah were in the courtyard below him. Jesus knew that most of them would never accept him and it would be their rejection of him that would lead to such suffering. Satan knew this as well.

"If You are the Son of God, throw Yourself down from here; for it is written, 'HE WILL COMMAND HIS ANGELS CONCERNING YOU TO GUARD YOU,' and, 'ON *their* HANDS THEY WILL BEAR YOU UP, SO THAT YOU WILL NOT STRIKE YOUR FOOT AGAINST A STONE.'" Satan said appealing to Jesus' pride.

Jesus knew what Satan was asking him to do. This temptation appealed to him on so many levels. It appealed to the universal human need for acceptance from one's peers. It appealed to his self-preservation instincts. It also appealed to his pride. Do this one thing and he would immediately not have to deal with all the nay-sayers and critics. Him falling from the temple and the sudden appearance of angels would proclaim to everyone present that he was the Messiah. The leaders of Israel would fall in behind him and the entire nation would accept him. But to do such a thing would not be about the Father and his will, but all about Jesus. Satan was appealing to his human pride and offering him another short cut. But this would not be in submission to the Father or the Father's will. This was not what Jesus wanted and so he answered Satan, "It is said, 'YOU SHALL NOT PUT THE LORD YOUR GOD TO THE TEST.'"

Suddenly Satan was gone and Jesus was back in the wilderness alone. Jesus knew that Satan would be back, but he also knew that he has resisted the three great temptations of life; the lust of the flesh, the lust of the eye, and the pride of life.

Jesus turned his gaze to the northwest; to Galilee. He would return there but things would be much different. For the man who went down to be baptized by John; the man upon whom the Holy Spirit had descended upon and then was led into the wilderness; the man Jesus Christ would return to the Galilee in the power of the Holy Spirit.

5. The Climax

At one time or another, we all find ourselves in a period of supernatural trial and temptation. We have been led into the wilderness and can't understand why these things are happening to us. Often we fail to realize these attacks are moments of supernatural testing. They are allowed by God to grow and mature us, to prove us, and to prepare us for the divine release of God's power in our lives.

These times are like a surprise pop quiz in school. You either are prepared or you are not. You will either pass or fail. Unfortunately, you can't go deeper into God until you pass the test.

How many times must we stumble and fall, failing the same test over and over, before we stop blaming Satan for his attack and realize the trial is God's opportunity for us to grow and mature.

6. Resolve (The Appeal)

Have you been wasting your trials and temptations? Do you find yourself in the same place with God, repeating the same tests over and over again? Have you lost hope and settled for mediocrity in your relationship with God?

God wants to empower each of us to do greater works than Jesus Christ himself. This is His will for you and me. But there are no shortcuts. If Jesus had to overcome temptation before he was filled with power, will we not have to do the same?

Today, my heart is challenged to renew my walk with Christ, to be filled with his Spirit, to be led by his Spirit, and to overcome temptation through the power of his Word.

How about you? Do you feel God calling you to follow Him? Would you raise your hand with me, acknowledging the need to renew our relationship and commitment to go deeper into Christ?

Perhaps you realize your relationship with God is broken and needs to be restored. I would like to lead you in a prayer to restore your relationship with God. Would you raise your hand, so that I can pray with you today?

Storytelling versus Teaching

What is the difference between preaching and teaching? There are many opinions regarding what differentiates one from the other, so here is yet another opinion.

- Preaching is designed to inspire the listener to do something.
- Teaching is designed to reveal truth and communicate understanding and knowledge.

When a minister speaks, it is almost never an "all-one-or-the-other" message. There is always a little teaching in the preaching and a little preaching in the teaching. Understanding our purpose helps us select the best tools to accomplish our goals.

If our intent is to provoke our audience to action, we will need more than just information or argument. Remember Madison Avenue advertising. Info ads inform and teach about products and benefits. Story ads move emotions and inspire the buyer to go and purchase a particular brand. In the same way, story based sermons have greater potential to move an audience to a desired response. Great evangelist have used stories to create powerful pictures of hell and eternity motivating the audience to respond to his appeal. Likewise, missionaries who are able to tell great stories that move the hearts of the congregation are more likely to receive a larger offering.

The following story has been told as an evangelism tool. As a result of this story, thousands of boys and girls have come to Christ.

Sample Story: Crusade Comes

Here is an interesting story that I have told in numerous locations to various types of audiences over the past 20 years. The story originally was created for a scouting type event with 5,500 men and boys sitting on a hillside. Most recently it was told around a campfire at the 2012 International Orality Network Conference in Estes Park, Colorado. The original story was almost 30 minutes in length. This is the 10 minute pared down version created for the ION Conference.

Crusader Comes

Lightning split the English countryside revealing the dark castle of the evil Duke Ravenhurst. A lone light burned in the east tower where Mercurial the Necromancer stood before his cauldron reciting incantations to speak with the dead. In the rafters above him, perched upon a massive oak timber, stood Ichbod the demon principality of the land. Once a creature of unsurpassed beauty, he now sprouted horns and bat like wings, which had been grafted into his head and shoulders. His naked body was covered in tattoos, each a blasphemous curse aimed at his creator. Hundreds of other lesser demons surrounded him. Some perched upon rafters, other hanging upside down as if bats.

Suddenly a small messenger demon burst through the roof and hovered in the air before him. With a lightning fast move the demon prince grabbed the messenger by the throat. "Well, what is it, worm?" He hissed. The small demon's eyes bulged as he whispered to the demon prince. Ichbod's yellow eyes narrowed as he heard the message. He shook the small demon until its eyes glazed over and then he tossed its limp body back through the very wall from which it had entered.

Then, unfurling his massive wings, Ichbod the demon prince of hell stepped off of the rafter and glided down to land upon the shoulders of the Mercurial the Necromancer. Spreading his talon like hand, he thrust it down into the head of the magician. Visions exploded in Mercurial's mind.

The door to his chamber burst open as Duke Ravenhurst entered. "Well, Mercurial, what is your word? Shall we defeat the Earl of Westbrook on the morrow?"

"Yes my Lord Ravenhurst, we will. But, be warned, there comes one who can defeat us. I have seen it in a vision. Beware, beware of the Crusader!"

Early the next morning, Robert carried his bow and quiver of arrows into the woods in search of game to place meat upon the table of his aging grandmother and younger brother, William. Although born noble, they all lived as peasants. Robert was 15 years of age but still battled nightmares. His sleep had once again been plagued by the horrific memories of parents murdered by a knight clad in black and red. The loss of his parents weighed heavily upon him. He remembered them. He remembered what it was like to live in a great manor. The nightmares would not let him forget. Yet again, another night of tortured sleep with another morning wishing he had died with his parents so many years ago. It was only for his brother William that he pasted a smile upon his face each day. His younger brother did not remember anything from their previous life and Robert had made a commitment that he would find a way to make things right for his young and innocent little brother.

The woods were silent. Not a single creature stirred. The morning pressed towards noon and Robert saw neither rabbit, partridge, or deer. Farther and farther from his grandmother's simple cottage he roamed in search of game. But the woods remained silent. Robert paused to listen. A strange distant sound made its way across the hillside and down to where he stood. Fascinated, Robert climbed to the top of the hill, the sound becoming louder and clearer with each step. Cresting the hill, Robert looked below to a most wondrous yet terrifying sight.

The valley spread out before him in low rolling pastures lined by thick woods. Two great armies stood ready to battle to the death. From his left came a massive army clad in black and red. On his right was the other in blue and yellow. Robert watched in fascination and horror as the two armies charged towards each other. They met in a sickening crash followed by cries of anger and pain mixed with the ringing of steel upon steel. Robert felt sorrow for the men in blue. They were obviously outnumbered and soon would be dead, leaving their wives as widows and their children fatherless.

Across the valley Ichbod the demon prince sat perched upon the shoulder of Mercurial. Duke Ravenhurst and Mercurial watched the battle from a hillside vantage point. Ravenhurst could taste victory. Mercurial was not so confident. Something in the spirit world was amiss and it left him uneasy.

Ichbod's demons circled in the sky above. Spirits of fear and despair sapped the Earl's army of their will to fight. Circling above them were the reapers. As the wicked and arrogant were struck a mortal blow, a reaper would dive out of the sky to land upon the chest of the dying. As the man breathed his last and closed his eyes to this mortal world, he would suddenly awake to the spirit world and be met by the clawed talons of the reaper who would then snatch the man's soul and drag it into the depths of hell. The cries of agony on the battlefield were but a whisper to the screams of utter terror from the dead facing their eternity.

As Robert watched from his hillside vantage a flash of white appeared at the edge of the distant forest. His body shook with excitement as he saw a knight in polished armor upon a white horse come racing out of the woods towards the battle. Without breaking stride he rode into the midst of the black army his sword cutting a path before him as a man might harvest wheat. The battle suddenly shifted as the Earl's men rallied around the white knight. But Ravenhurst had not grown powerful being a fool. From the opposite side of the woods appeared another thousand soldiers clad in black and red rushing towards the flank of the Earl's battle line cutting it in two. Suddenly the white knight found himself with a small company of the Earl's men cut off from the battle and being pushed back into a small clearing at the base of a hill.

Robert stood upon that very hillside and watched in horror as the battle suddenly unfolded just below him. The brave knight was clearly in danger of being overwhelmed. It would take a miracle for the knight to survive. Without thinking Robert reached into his quiver and pulled an arrow. With one smooth movement he knocked the arrow to the string, drew it back to his cheek, and then released it. An attacker fell as it found its mark. Robert took a few steps down the hillside as he drew another arrow and let it fly. Within a minute Robert's quiver was empty and he found himself standing at the bottom of the hill with the battle just a few yards in front of him. Dropping his bow and quiver he ran towards the battle picking up a small shield and short sword from the body of a dead soldier. A moment later he found himself standing shoulder to shoulder with the white knight and fighting for his life. Robert had no idea what he was doing. He blocked spear thrusts and hacked at the men in black trying to protect both the knight and himself. Robert heard the distinct sound of an arrow zip by him. Scanning the clearing he saw the archer drawing another arrow to his cheek. Without a thought of fear or doubt he leapt in front of the knight. The arrow sped across the clearing seeking its mark and then buried itself into Robert's chest.

The demons of hell cried out in glee as they tasted victory! But suddenly in the midst of their blackness exploded a brilliant flash of light and where there had been nothing a moment before appeared a hundred angels of the heavenly host, standing shoulder to shoulder with blazing swords drawn forming a circle around the knight and fallen boy. The demons shrieked in fear as they clawed their way back into the sky.

Without apparent explanation, a sudden overwhelming dread fell upon the black and red soldiers of Duke Ravenhurst. Spinning about they dropped their weapons and fled from the clearing trampling over the dead and dying. Then, there was silence. The white knight stood alone in the clearing, his surcoat slashed and splattered with blood. Sheathing his sword and then lifting his great helm from his head, he knelt beside Robert cradling him in his arms. "You have shown me a great kindness, lad," the knight said tenderly. "Is there no one in your family I can reward on your behalf?"

Robert looked into the rugged face of the knight. Coldness was already creeping into his arms and legs. "I have a brother . . . William," Robert gasped.

"Then I will find your brother William, and make him my squire," the knight said.

The demons recovered from the surprise appearance of the Host. Ichbod himself had risen into the air gathering his demon army for a battle. The Host, outnumbered 1000 to 1, stood gallantly awaiting the black onslaught, their swords raised to the sky. Then, in unison, they all sank to their knees and bowed. A blast of searing white light, more brilliant than a hundred suns exploded in their midst, the blast blinding the demon hoard sending them shrieking in painful retreat. And then there, standing in the midst of the angels was the Captain of the Host, the creator of the Universe, Jesus Christ the Son of the living God. And as Robert breathed his last and closed his eyes to this world, he opened them into the spirit world to be greeted by his Lord and Savior.

"Robert, are you ready to go home? Your parents are waiting for you," Jesus said with a smile.

"But, what of William?" Robert asked.

"Ah, your brother has his own destiny to fulfill. He must become the crusader to deliver this land from darkness. Come." And as Jesus wrapped his arms around Robert, together with the Host singing praise to God Almighty they shot upward in a beam of pure light, out of this world and into the presence of God.